HEARING THE WORD SERIES

Teaching the BIBLE IN THE PARISH (AND BEYOND)

The 2010 Hein-Fry Lectures
Series XX

Laurie Jungling, editor

Lutheran University Press
Minneapolis, Minnesota

Teaching the Bible in the Parish (and Beyond)

HEARING THE WORD SERIES

The 2010 Hein-Fry Lectures • Series XX

Laurie Jungling, editor

Copyright 2011 Lutheran University Press, an imprint of 1517 Media. All rights reserved. Expect for brief quotations in articles or reviews, no part of this book may be reproduced in any manner without written permission of the publisher: 1517 Media Permissions, PO Box 1209, Minneapolis, MN 55440-1209, or copyright@1517.media.

Library of Congress Cataloging-in-Publication Data

Teaching the Bible in the parish (and beyond) : the 2010 Hein-Fry lectures / Laurie Jungling, editor.

   p. cm. – (Hearing the word series ; ser. 20)

   ISBN-13: 978-1-932688-58-0 (alk. paper)

   ISBN-10: 1-932688-58-7 (alk. paper)

   eISBN: 978-1-942304-82-1

   1. Bible--Study and teaching--Evangelical Lutheran Church in America. I. Jungling, Laurie. II. Title: 2010 Hein-Fry lectures.

BS588.E93T43 2011

220.071--dc22

2011008222

Table of Contents

Foreword 5

Preface 7

Introduction 9
    Richard A. Jensen

Encountering Jesus in the River of Scripture 11
    Susan Briehl

Communicating the Word in the Congregation 27
    Margaret A. Krych

Enacted Utterances: Tracing the Power of the Divine in Luke 46
    Richard Carlson

Recovering the Bible as Oral Performances in Community 65
    David Rhoads

Learning the Bible in the Twenty-first Century:
Lessons from Harry Potter and Vampires 79
    Mary Hess

The Lecturers 100

Foreword

The Hein-Fry Lecture Series

The annual Hein-Fry Lecture Series is the premier endowed theological lecture series of the Evangelical Lutheran Church in America (ELCA). For the annual series, the governing committee identifies lively, pressing theological issues facing the church. The lectures, traditionally delivered at the eight ELCA seminaries, are free and open to the public.

The goals of the lecture series are to:

- foster original scholarship,
- encourage broad dialogue throughout the church on a theological topic, and
- give seminary faculty, students, clergy, church leaders, and other interested persons access to leading theologians.

The Hein Fry Lecture Series grows out of prestigious traditions dating back more than fifty years in the histories of the ELCA predecessor church bodies.

The Hein Lectures were first held at the American Lutheran Church seminary in Columbus, Ohio. After 1960 the Hein Seminary Lectures were held each year at the four seminaries of the American Lutheran Church. The Fry Lectures continue and expand on the series known as Knubel-Miller-Greever Lectures, which were held at various seminaries and other locations of the Lutheran Church in America.

The Hein-Fry Lecture Series is unique in that it addresses all the seminary communities within a major American denomination. This gives the series great potential for engaging both the current theological leadership and a generation of ministerial candidates in discussion of a focused theological issue.

This lecture series was coordinated by the Vocation and Education unit of the Evangelical Lutheran Church in America. Lecture topics, speakers, and schedules were set by the Hein-Fry Lecture Series Governing Committee:*

Rev. Jessica Crist
> Northern Rockies Institute of Theology, Great Falls, Montana

Dr. Duane Larson
> Wartburg Theological Seminary, Dubuque, Iowa

Bishop Robert Hofstad
> Southwestern Washington Synod, Tacoma, Washington

Dean Donald Huber
> Trinity Lutheran Seminary, Columbus, Ohio

Rev. Jana Schofield
> Mount Carmel Lutheran Church, San Luis Obispo, California

Ms. Carolyn Wright
> Program Committee, ELCA Vocation and Education, Fargo, North Dakota

Rev. Dr. Jonathan P. Strandjord
> Director of Theological Education, ELCA Vocation and Education, Chicago, Illinois

Rev. Laurie Jungling, Ph.D.
> Hein-Fry Lecture Series Administrator, ELCA Vocation and Education, Great Falls, Montana

* Note: *the names and positions of the members of the governing committee are reflective of the time in which the committee made the decisions regard this series of lectures.*

Preface

Hearing the Word!

In August 2007, the Churchwide Assembly of the Evangelical Lutheran Church in America approved a major initiative entitled Book of Faith: Lutherans Read the Bible. This initiative has the goal of "raising to a new level this church's individual and collective engagement with the Bible and its teaching, yielding greater biblical fluency and a more profound appreciation of Lutheran principles and approaches for the use of Scripture." In a desire to participate in the advancement of the ELCA's Book of Faith initiative, the Hein-Fry Governing Committee developed a three-year sequence for the Hein-Fry Lectures entitled "Hearing the Word."

The specific topics for this three-year sequence are:

- 2009—"Hearing the Word: Lutheran Perspectives on Biblical Interpretation"
- 2010—"Hearing the Word: Teaching the Bible in the Parish (and Beyond)"
- 2011—"Hearing the Word: Lutherans Read the Bible with the Ecumenical World"

The 2010 Lecture Series

> Day after day, in the temple courts and from house to house, they never stopped teaching and proclaiming the good news that Jesus is the Christ (Acts 5:42, NIV).

The Hein-Fry lecture topic for 2010 was "Hearing the Word: Teaching the Bible in the Parish (and Beyond)." This theme was chosen in order to explore the important conversations throughout the ELCA concerning the various ways Lutheran communities in diverse North American contexts are sharing the biblical narratives, truths, and messages of the gospel through their teaching ministries. The hope for these presentations is that they will raise awareness about the many ways the Lutheran churches have traditionally taught the Bible as well as offer innovative contemporary approaches to teaching the Bible that Lutherans might use today.

Five scholars affiliated with the ELCA were invited to offer lectures out of their particular perspectives and scholarship. Each lecturer traveled to three sites where he or she delivered a major presentation exploring important and innovative Lutheran perspectives on biblical interpretation, making a case for the promise of one, some, or even all of them. At most of the sites, a local respondent reflected in a second session to the traveling lecturer's presentation in light of its relevance to the regional context. A third session brought the two speakers into conversation with each other and the audience.

The Hein-Fry lectures for 2010 took place between February and April 2010. In order to expand the reach of this important conversation, the committee elected to bring the lectures to seven sites in addition to the eight ELCA seminaries traditionally visited. These new sites included four ELCA-affiliated colleges and three congregational forums in areas of the country not easily served by the eight seminaries. Thus, the Hein-Fry lectures were delivered at a total of fifteen sites in 2010.

Introduction

This series of Hein-Fry Lectures turns to a very practical matter. You should expect to find here new approaches to the teaching of the Bible in your parish (and beyond). These fine lectures offer a variety of angles on this topic. The ELCA is to be commended for bending this year's lectures toward practical parish reality.

Susan Briehl invites us to new ways of hearing God's Word. She claims to be sharing with us her pastoral wisdom on the matter. Her article contains a solid Lutheran foundation and some very helpful teaching tools. The teaching tools she suggests could well be shared with all who teach the Bible in a parish context. There is some wonderful wisdom here!

Margaret Krych's article is a good companion piece to that by Briehl. Krych grasps well the distinctively Lutheran foundations of what we are to be about in our teaching. She asserts, for example, that ultimately hearing the Word is hearing Christ. I found this to be a very helpful and practical lecture. This chapter could also be shared with the teachers of Scripture in the congregation.

The lecture by Richard Carlson, a New Testament professor, plunges us into the world of biblical study. In his lecture he wants us to grasp the "worlds" of the biblical texts: the World Behind the Text; the World of the Biblical Text and the World in Front of the Text. Carlson helps us grasp these worlds through a study of the Greek word *rhēma in Luke's gospel.* His study unites theory and practice. He demonstrates his point by looking at Luke 1:5-38; 5:1-11; 24:1-12. In these texts a *rhēma* of God is addressed to Mary, the disciples and the women at the tomb. Their response is a response of faith in the promissory word of God. We, too, are called to respond in faith to the promissory *rhēma* of God. There is much help in a study like this for our teaching and our preaching.

David Rhoads has been a pioneer in the practice of oral performance—the recitation of Scripture passages by memory. Hearing the biblical stories in this manner breaks open incredible new possibilities of meaning. For example, when I first heard Dr. Rhoads recite the Gospel of Mark, I understood the ending of Mark's gospel for the first time. When I heard it, I got it! Mark's gospel ended in my heart! The gospel ends with the fear of the women at the startling news of resurrection. The thought flashed through my mind as I heard this ending: "Am I afraid?" What is my response to Mark's Jesus? I would urge you to learn from David Rhoads and make Bible storytelling an important aspect of your parish life Your people can hear these stories. Your people can tell these stories.

Finally there is a lecture by Mary Hess with the provocative title, "Lessons From Harry Potter and the Vampires." She asserts that she is offering us a way of seeing that will help us more adequately construct a prescription for our context. She is interested in helping us learn the Bible in a media culture. Her references to particular aspects of our media culture and her zeal to help us navigate this culture in our teaching of the Bible speak to important aspects of our teaching challenge in today's world.

Richard A. Jensen
Lutheran School of Theology at Chicago, *emeritus*

Encountering Jesus in the River of Scripture

Susan Briehl
Valparaiso University

Since 1988 the Hein-Fry Lecture series has sought to foster original scholarship among the finest teachers of the church and thus enrich theological dialogue throughout the church. This year, however, at least as evidenced in their invitation to me, the committee had something else in mind when they chose the theme, "Hearing the Word: Teaching the Bible in the Parish and Beyond." What I share with you might best be called pastoral wisdom. It rises from my reading, studying, and teaching the Bible as a Lutheran pastor, or better, from nurturing deeper engagement with the Word of God through Scripture, in the parish and beyond. Beyond, in my case, means among students on college campuses and seminarians in preaching classes, with confirmands on retreat and catechumens in prison, as a member of an intentional Christian community, and in the company of other preachers and teachers.

The adventure of studying Scripture began in earnest for me as an undergraduate at a state university in a course called The Bible as Literature. On the first day of class a tall, dignified, white-haired man walked in and proclaimed, "The subject is the Bible, and I am the Lord! Professor Jack Lord." We dug into the Bible using all of the literary critical methods we were learning as English majors, methods meant to help us read a text closely and critically for what it is saying and doing: discerning genre, tracing sources, noting syntax and grammar and style, unpacking thick descriptions, exploring images. We mapped the plot, analyzed characters—both flat and round—paid attention to setting and voice and point of view, and honed our skills at catching and understanding irony, metaphor, symbolism, allusion, and the like. Maybe only another English major can imagine how much fun this was.

Professor Lord gave me one of the greatest gifts of my life: the invitation to study Scripture using every exegetical tool available to me, the permission to bring my own gifts and interests and curiosities to the task. I want to make the same invitation and give the same permission to you and others, for during that semester this book, which I thought I knew having grown up in the church, opened its portals to reveal unimagined treasure, and continued to open thus throughout my graduate studies in literary history and criticism. Luther was right, I would have said in those years, if I had known in those years that Luther wrote this, Scripture is "the richest of mines which can never be sufficiently explored."[1] The adventure, the exploration, the discovery, and the delight have yet to cease.

Not everyone has such positive experiences with the Bible. Take Huckleberry Finn for example. "After supper," Huck says, [the Widow Douglas] "got out her book and learned me about Moses and the Bulrushers; and I was in a sweat to find out all about him; but by-and-by she let out that Moses had been dead a considerable long time; so then I didn't care no more about him; because I don't take stock in dead people."[2]

A dead word about dead people, that's what Huck Finn heard from the "good book," a book full of rules meant to "sivilize" him, but not a word that had anything to do with his real life, his fear of death, his dreams of freedom, or his friendship with Jim, the run-away slave, forged through flood and fog on the mighty Mississippi River.

But the undergraduate English major also ran the risk of hearing only a dead word as she headed into the treasure trove of this ancient library with her excavating tools in hand, ready to mine its deepest riches, hoping to uncover clues, solve its riddles, and emerge victorious with the "truth" in hand, as if truth were a thing to be grasped and claimed and graded. As long as she examined and evaluated these texts simply as archeological artifacts or great literature, the words could stay on the page, complicated, intriguing, even inspiring, but ultimately disconnected from the heart of her life.

Lambs and Elephants: A Variety of Readers

A thousand years before Luther described Scripture as a mine, Gregory the Great likened it to a river. Gregory had been working on what he called "An Exposition on the Book of Beloved Job," when he wrote in a letter to his fellow bishop, Leander, that the Word of God, is

> a kind of river . . . which is both shallow and deep,
> in which the lamb might find a footing,
> and the elephant float at large.[3]

Imagine that. Scripture as a river shallow enough for those who are wading in like children, reading, hearing, studying it for the first time, or for the first time in a long time. If your experience is anything like mine, this will be good news to you and to others in the places you worship and serve.

Consider how varied these readers and hearers of the Word are. Seekers come full of curiosity about this book and, like Huck was at first, all "in a sweat" to find out more. The anxious worry that they might lose their footing if they wade in too far and what they long have held as true is swept out from beneath them by swift currents, their whole worldview washed away. Those who have put away what they judge to be an outgrown, inadequate faith, wonder if the B-I-B-L-E, about which they sang as children, holds anything substantial enough to nurture an adult faith in a complicated, compromised, pluralistic world. Still others, including some life-long Lutheran Christians are a little embarrassed (even defensive) about what they do not know, about how little they have read and studied the Bible as adults. And the wounded, bearing scars of pain inflicted or justified by the misuse of Scripture, are scared to death of the water. All of these might be numbered among the lambs that come to the river to drink and are promised a footing.

Then picture the elephants: Believers steeped in Scripture through years of devotional reading and prayer, the very fabric of their lives woven of biblical images and wisdom. Attentive hearers of the Word as it is read and preached, sung and enacted in the worshipping assembly week after week, who engage the whole world through biblically formed imaginations. And muscular wrestlers with the Word, who like Jacob limp away from their life and death struggle on the banks of the river, weary and wet with sweat, but glistening with God's blessing. The waters of Scripture, Gregory assures such elephants, are deep enough for you; neither the most learned scholar nor the life-long student will ever plumb its depths.

All of these readers and more could be part of your circle of friends, your community of faith, the little band that gathers to open the Bible together. How might you welcome them as they come, each with his or her own particular history with the Bible? What might you do to make room in the conversation for each of them?

Welcome to the River

One way to welcome a rich diversity of persons to open Scripture together is to give them sure footing on common ground: offer them a shared working description of the Word of God. Here is one idea. Place before them the three-fold definition of the Word of God from the ELCA constitution, a clear, concise confession of faith that

- First, "Jesus Christ is the Word of God incarnate, through whom everything was made and through whose life, death, and resurrection God fashions a new creation."

- Second, "The proclamation of God's message to us as both Law and Gospel is the Word of God, revealing judgment and mercy through word and deed, beginning with the Word in creation, continuing in the history of Israel, and centering in all its fullness in the person and work of Jesus Christ."

- And third, "The canonical Scriptures of the Old and New Testaments are the written Word of God. Inspired by God's Spirit speaking through their authors, they record and announce God's revelation centering in Jesus Christ. Through them God's Spirit speaks to us to create and sustain Christian faith and fellowship for service in the world."[4]

In one congregation a calligrapher has created a beautiful, briefer version of this on rice paper and hung it on the wall of the parish hall as both a teaching tool and a testimony:

> Jesus Christ
> is the Word of God incarnate;
> God's message of judgment and mercy
> is the Word of God proclaimed and heard;
> Holy Scripture is the written
> Word of God.

Consider another way to welcome an eclectic gathering of elephants and lambs and everything in between to the study of Scripture. Invite them to this book as you would to the baptismal font or the communion table, for here too is a means of grace, here too Christ promises to meet us with the gifts of mercy and life. Here too something finite and earthly bears to us what is infinite and eternal, not bread and wine or water, but words. Human language is imperfect and imprecise, words are slippery and insufficient. Even so we ask these flawed little vessels—these "precious cups of meaning,"[5] as Saint Augustine called them—to hold the unbearable weight of all we long to say and all we need to hear.

And to such finite things God entrusts the holy, eternal Word. Human words become *Theotokas*, vessels that bear God to the world. Through these stories and songs, genealogies and histories, fables, parables and prophetic utterances, letters and liturgies, God's creative Spirit broods and breathes, calling forth faith and forming a people for the sake of the world. In, with, and under these words Christ meets us "that we may have life and have it abundantly" (John 10:10). "Welcome," you might say, "to the river of mercy flowing from the heart of God; welcome to Christ Jesus. Let's wade in."

Wading In

When reading the Bible, start at the beginning and stop at the end. I do not mean reading from the "In the beginning" of Genesis 1:1 to the "Amen" of Revelation 22:21. I mean as you prepare, and perhaps as you lead, first read the entire section of Scripture that you will be studying. Read the whole epistle, the whole psalm, the entire gospel, or minor prophet, or creation narrative. Do not labor or linger over things; let the narrative move you along. If a question arises in your mind, with a pencil make a little question mark in the margin. If something surprises or strikes you, make an explanation point. Draw a heart next to a line you want to commit to memory. As one scholar suggests, put an asterisk wherever you think there should be a footnote. And so forth. My Bibles are riddled with such tiny hieroglyphics legible only to me. In preparing to preach or teach, this practice helps us maintain a sense of the whole even as we study the details of each part. This is a basic Lutheran principle for reading the Bible; each verse is understood in the context of the passage, each passage in the context of the book, each book in the context of the canon. So, begin at the beginning and end at the end.

Getting Your Bearings

Entering any story, readers need to get their bearings, to figure out where and when the story is set. Though the character Huck Finn was not helped much by the Good Book, the novel *Huckleberry Finn* might help readers of Scripture understand the distinction between setting and audience. By that I mean simply that the place and time in which a story is set may or may not reflect the time and place of the audience for which it first was written.

The story of Huckleberry Finn begins in St. Petersburg, Missouri, a fictional river town, sometime in the mid-1800s when slavery was the law of the land in the South. But Mark Twain did not write it as an anti-slavery novel. He did not have to; he wrote it twenty years *after* Abraham Lincoln signed the Emancipation Proclamation of 1863. Twain's intended audience, the first readers, lived during Reconstruction, an era shaped by federal policies meant to integrate freed slaves into society, rebuild the South, and mend the Union following the Civil War. During this time racism and fear, too deeply woven into the fabric of human hearts and communities to be abolished by legislation, grew more subtle, more sinister. So Twain told a story set in the past in order to shed light on the hypocrisy and oppression of the present. We who read the novel today are not Twain's intended audience. Knowing and remembering that helps us enter and hear the story more deeply, even though it might still shed light upon us and our time.

Much the same is true when we read the Bible. While in prison in Rome or Ephesus, Paul wrote his letter to Philemon, who lived in Colossae. In this case the author, the writing, and the intended audience all belong to a common time and place. The great hymn of creation in Genesis 1, however, wasn't written "in the beginning," but during the Babylonian exile when the children of Israel, cut off from their homes and their sacred places, now in ruins, could no longer "sing the songs of Zion." There and then faithful poets wrote a new song for the strangers in a strange land to sing, a song of the God whose word brings order from chaos; whose love creates out of nothing, everything good. "As it was in the beginning, so it is now," they sang in trust and hope, "God's word has the power to make a new creation, even here, even now in the midst of our desolation."

The four gospels, set in Palestine during Jesus' lifetime, were written from and for faith communities living four or five or more decades after his death and resurrection. The evangelists wrote the Good News, set in the past, but for the sake of the present. While telling the story of Jesus, they were speaking to the fears and hopes and struggles that their contemporaries were facing. Sometimes, getting these bearings is enough to launch readers into a very present-tense encounter with the Word.

Charting the Course

Sometimes more tools are useful. So let me introduce you to a quirky method of exploring this inexhaustible mine, of wading into the river of Scripture, then diving ever more deeply down. It requires some imagination and involves long strips of adding machine tape and colored markers, a decidedly low-tech approach with many higher-tech possibilities. Sometimes I do all or part of this in advance of leading a Bible study, at other times it is a group activity, a hands-on approach to opening Scripture.

On the first strip of adding machine tape simply mark and number the chapters. If you allocate six inches for each chapter, the gospel according to Luke is twelve feet long, and the Acts of the Apostles is another fourteen! Whatever the book, whatever the length, if you affix this first strip to a wall, you will be able to place additional strips of adding machine tape beneath it, layer after layer, until you have something that looks like the geological strata on the sides of the Grand Canyon.

On that first strip of paper or another, mark the major sections of the work you are studying. For instance, if you were charting the entire book of Genesis, you might follow Walter Brueggemann's lead and mark and name four major sections: The Pre-History(1:1—11:9), The Abraham Narrative (11:30—25:18); The Jacob Narrative (25:19—36:43); and The Joseph Narrative (37:1—50:26).[6] This creates a visual picture of the basic structure of a book or narrative.

On the next strip of paper, lined up under the first two, note discrete stories, episodes, events, and give them titles. Under the section of Genesis labeled the Pre-History you again might follow Brueggemann and write Creation of the World (1:-2:4); Creation and Rebellion of Humankind (2:4b—3:24); Expulsion of Cain (4); Genealogy from Creation to the Flood (5). Or better, the group might together read these passages and name them. This is nothing more than scholars do in their commentaries and many editions of the Bible offer with their headings at the top of the page. But giving the episodes titles is itself an interpretive task and can draw readers into lively engagement with the text and one another.

If you were studying the Gospel of Luke together, after reading the beloved parable in chapter 15, ask, what would be a good title for this parable? Or you could ask, shall we call it The Prodigal Son or The Righteous Son? Or set in the context of the whole chapter with The Lost Sheep and The Lost Coin, shall we do as Eugene Peterson does and call it The Lost Brothers?[7] How does our hearing of the Word change if with Helmut Thielicke we call it The Waiting Father?[8] Or with Kenneth Bailey call it The Running Father?[9] The lambs often lead the elephants in this interpretive task. Those who are less familiar with the stories are sometimes more curious, more insightful, because they are less bound to what they think they already know is true.

Identifying Genres

On the next strip of paper identify genres. Now you are swimming into new territory for many and may need to explain what we mean by genre—a specific type of literature, marked by a particular form or style or content—and why it matters whether we are reading a parable, a proverb, a call narrative, a hymn, or a letter. Remember that there are genres inside genres. Romans is a letter or an epistle, with its to-be-expected opening greeting and prayer of thanksgiving and its closing greetings and blessing. But inside this letter are theological arguments, rhetorical questions, exhortations, and analogies. Paul quotes passages from the Psalms and the prophets frequently, and every once in a while breaks into a rapturous song of praise. All of these genres and more comprise what we call Paul's letter to the Romans.

Now compare Romans, a letter written for the sake of the whole Church, to the very brief, personal letter that Paul writes from prison to Philemon and Apphia and the church in their house. He makes a heartfelt plea to them to forgive and receive as their brother, the slave Onesimus, who has become like a child to Paul. This "occasional letter," written for a specific occasion, audience, and purpose draws in even a very young reader with its immediacy and transparency, its familiar form and final request, "Oh, and one more thing—prepare a guestroom for me." Identifying the genre or genres of a given work helps the reader know how to approach the text, how to hear most clearly what it is saying and doing, and how God is still speaking in and through it.

Surveying the Landscape

Sometimes I include a strip on which to chart journeys and geography and places. Many of us grew up with maps of Paul's travels hanging in the church fellowship room or the circuitous routes of Israel's forty-year sojourn in the wilderness in the back of our Bibles, but few of us learned to track other journeys or note less obvious places. Sometimes going "into the wilderness" or "up the mountain" or to "a place apart" is not so much about locating a spot on a map as it is about an encounter with God or a journey of the heart or the shaping of a community. In Luke's gospel people are forever being sent "home" or returning "home" or receiving Jesus into their "homes." What is happening at home? Is it only where one dwells, or is it for Luke the place where grace abides and the household of faith flourishes?

And what might it mean in Luke that Jesus' first journey is to the temple in Jerusalem as an infant and that his life's journey ends in Jerusalem too? Or that he begins his ministry in Galilee, but when he sets his face toward Jerusalem and the cross, the whole narrative slows down, almost to real time, as he walks through the foreign territory of Samaria? Or that after encountering the risen Christ in their "home" in Emmaus, the disciples immediately return to Jerusalem? Having come to the end of the twelve-foot tape of Luke, we are ready for the fourteen-foot tape of Acts where, once again, Jerusalem is Jerusalem, and so much more.

A group of eighth and ninth graders, mapping Mark's gospel, were fascinated to watch Jesus getting in and out of a boat crossing to one side of the Sea of Galilee and then to the other, weaving like a drunken sailor, as one kid said, as he traced the movement on the adding machine tape. Together we asked, "What is going on here? What is Jesus up to? And why? What might the people on either side of the sea have made of this sailing back and forth, casting out demons first on one side (1:21-28) then on the other (5:10-20), healing a bleeding woman and raising a little girl to life on one side (5:22-43), then healing a little girl and a deaf man on the other (7:24-37), feeding a multitude and teaching first here (6:32-44), then there (8:1-10), as if to stitch the sides together with the running thread of his words and deeds. Not to mention the amazing things he did smack dab in the middle of the sea (4:35—5:1 and 6:45-53). Together we wonder: Where in the world is Christ making these crossings today?

Following the Action

On another strip, trace the movement of the narrative, the storyline or plot. Follow those verbs, I tell readers of Scripture—that is where the action is. When charting the course of John's gospel one time, someone noticed that at several pivotal points the narrator reports on how people respond to something Jesus says or does. Early in the gospel the narrator reports, "His disciples believed in him" (2:11), then, "Many believed in his name" (2:23). A few chapters later the plot turns as we hear that "many of his disciples turned back and no longer went about with him" (6:66). Then we learn that some began to report on Jesus to the authorities, and finally, others "from that day on . . . planned to put him to death" (11:53). We had to ask: What evokes these responses? Why do both devotion to and antagonism against Jesus increase? Where does this deepening divide take the story? The characters? The first readers? Us? How does it more fully reveal the one sent from God?

Oh, you get the idea. You could create tapes that kept track of the characters, or recurring images or motifs, or the phrases or words particular to the book you are reading. You could explore all of the places it quotes, or alludes to, or uses images from other biblical passages. You will think of things I never imagined.

After creating these strips, I roll them, tie them with string, and put them in small boxes. My little Jonah box has eight strips; Philippians has six. My Gospel of John box has more than a dozen. When they are all taped on a wall or on a long table, one below the next, a person can read the text horizontally, from its beginning to its end. But a person also can read it vertically, wading in, then diving more deeply into a single scene.

Reading Again and Again

In the first parish that I served, fresh from seminary, I prepared to offer an adult Bible study course in John's gospel. I created a stunning bulletin board announcing the class and inviting everyone to "An Encounter with Jesus." In the narthex that Sunday morning I watched as Russell and

Margaret, faithful elders in the congregation, stood admiring the bulletin board. "Ah, too bad," Russ said, more loudly than he meant to. "It's on John. We've already read that one."

"Those who read the gospel [according to John] for the first time," Craig Koester writes, "often find its meaning to be rather obvious." Then he adds, "the complexity and richness become increasingly apparent with rereading." The gospel's message, Koester continues, "is accessible at a basic level to less-informed readers, yet sophisticated enough to engage those who are better informed."[10] Koester is referring not to us, but to the first readers, the original hearers of the Word for whom John's gospel was written. The so-called "better informed" readers were Jewish Christians. Deeply formed in the teaching and tradition of Judaism, they could appreciate and apprehend the many-layered meanings of the metaphors, the thick symbolism, and rich scriptural allusions in the text.

The "less-informed readers" were outside this tradition, more recent members of the community—Samaritans and Greeks. In order to understand the basic message of the gospel and its particular Johannine claims, these readers needed some things explained to them, images opened up, words defined, practices unpacked, the "back story" told. The evangelist does all of these things through the literary device of a narrator.

The narrator is the voice that tells the story, sings the psalm, recounts the history, or describes the vision. Literary critics would describe the narrator in John as *reliable*, meaning the reader can trust him, and *omniscient*, meaning the narrator knows everything. He knows more than any other character in the story, except Jesus.[11] And he tells the readers, so that they are "in the know." This technique gives even the less-informed reader a privileged perspective from which to witness the unfolding drama. Even the "outsider" now has a place "inside" the story.

Like the Stage Manager in Thornton Wilder's "Our Town," the narrator of John breaks the frame of the story, steps out to the edge of the stage as it were, and speaks directly to the audience in little asides. He translates a term here: "'Rabbi' (which translated means Teacher)" (1:38). He provides an explanation there: "Judas Iscariot, one of the disciples (the one who was about to betray him)" (12:4). When some in the audience do not see what the big deal is when Jesus asks the woman at the well for a drink—because they do not know the complicated history of the political, ethnic, liturgical, biblical, theological divides between Jews and Samaritans—the narrator briefly turns toward them and says parenthetically, "Jews do not share things in common with Samaritans" (4:9). This comment does not tell them everything that is at work in this scene, but it tells them enough for them to understand the heart of this encounter at the well: Jesus is breaking barriers, shattering expectations, building new relationships as he widens his invitation to "come and see."[12]

The distance between today's reader and the original audience is vast. In this respect we are truly the "outsiders." Scholars are continually trying to unearth, recover, and piece together the histories, geographies, economies, worldviews, customs, and practices of the peoples through whom and for whom the biblical texts first came to be. As best we can, we seek to know how those first hearers and readers of the texts understood them. We start there so that we do not unwittingly superimpose our worldviews on to the text. This too is a classic Lutheran principle for reading Scripture.

So, in some cases you will take up a role akin to John's narrator or Wilder's Stage Manager when you prepare to facilitate or lead a Bible study. This is not a starring role. Relieved of the burden of appearing omniscient, you can pray to be a reliable guide. Your task is to discern what kind of information your community might need in order to understand the plain or literal meaning of the text, the meaning the first hearers might have heard, and then to make that information available. You can encourage and equip participants to use appropriate resources in their own further inquiry: a good study Bible, biblical dictionaries, maps, concordances, commentaries, and the like. You will bring to this task the tools and skills you have honed in your studies. For what we learn and unlearn in seminary (and beyond) is not our private treasure, it is part of the wealth of the Church, and we are called to pour it out generously, humbly wherever we serve.

One scholar describes the narrator in John as "winsomely intrusive;"[13] meaning, I think, that he inserts himself into the experience of the readers, but only when necessary, only when he knows something that will be helpful, and always with good humor and grace, standing beside, not above the readers. Not a bad role model for those of us who lead and nurture Scripture study.

Creating Community

There is even more at work here. Dive a little more deeply into the story of Jesus and the woman at the well. Imagine the original audience hearing this story. The scene is set in motion: Jesus leaves Judea with his disciples, heads toward Galilee, has to go through Samaria, stops at a town called Sychar at Jacob's well. See at work behind this scene, other biblical wells: the place of match making (Genesis 24) and meeting (Genesis 29:1-12), of divine provision and life-saving discovery (Genesis 21:15-19).

It is noon. The characters are in place. Jesus, tired out by the journey, sits by the well. A local woman, coming to draw water, enters stage right. Where are the disciples who were traveling with Jesus? The narrator dispatches them by turning toward the audience and whispering, "His disciples had gone to the city to buy food" (4:8). Exit stage left. Only these two remain: Jesus and the woman.

Oh, the narrator telling the story is there too, standing to the side, cluing in the "less-informed." Wait. The reader, the audience, is also present, watching the whole thing unfold, listening in on this "private" conversation.

Jesus says to the woman, "Give me a drink."

Hear the sharp intake of breath by those in the audience who know what this entails. They shake their heads, "Just a minute, Jesus, you are in forbidden territory. You are a Rabbi; she is a woman. You are a Jew; she is a Samaritan."

As if reading their minds, the woman asks Jesus, "How is it that you, a Jew, ask a drink of me, a woman of Samaria?" (John 4:9).

The Samaritans in the audience nod, thinking, "Pretty cheeky for a guy whose people so despise us that they insinuate that our women start menstruating when they are infants, unclean from the cradle, impure all of their lives." [14]

And before the less-informed—the Greeks, maybe, or children who do not know this history—can ask "What is the big deal? The man is thirsty, she has the vessel," the narrator makes the aside, "Jews do not share things in common with Samaritans."

But then imagine this, the members of the audience look around, to their right, to their left, across the table, and what do they see? One another: Palestinian Jews, Samaritans, Greeks, women, men, children. The story of the remarkable, irregular encounter between Jesus and the Samaritan woman is embodied, enacted in their company. *They* are the beloved community "born of water and the Spirit" (John 3:5), living testimony that in Christ the long-standing walls that once divided them are dismantled. *They* are the thirsty who have received the living water of Christ's word, the gift of the Spirit springing forth within and among them, well supplying them with life abundant. The evangelist tells the story not only in a way that makes it accessible to the whole spectrum of readers in its first audience, but also, in so doing, forms from this diverse gathering, one community, branches abiding in the same Vine (John 15:5).

And not only for the first hearers and readers of John, but every time people open Scripture together a community is being formed. The Holy Spirit calls and gathers them, teaches and enlightens them. The spectrum of readers is broader today than ever before, but still, we confess, this ancient river, these fragile, finite, fallible human words bear to us the Living Word of God, Jesus Christ. Here "God's Spirit speaks to us to create and sustain Christian faith and fellowship for service in the world."[15]

A pastor wiser than I, upon hearing Russell's comment to Margaret as they stood before the beautiful bulletin board, would have immediately, personally invited them to join the study—not only so they could discover the riches of reading John a second time, but also so they could accompany others who would be reading it for the first time. This is wisdom we receive from the catechumenate, that ancient, deliberate process of preparing candidates for baptism: beside every candidate a sponsor walks; an elephant accompanies each lamb to the water. This accompaniment, however, is not only for the sake of the lambs. As with every elephant, Russ and Margaret could step time and again into the river of John's gospel or any other part of Scripture for that matter, diving ever more deeply into its meaning, entering its narrative, accepting its invitation to "come and see," and expecting in faith to encounter God's living and life-giving Word.

Dying and Rising

A dead word about dead people—that is what Huck Finn heard. Truth—that is what the English major hoped to find. But the truth of the Bible is not offered to us in answers we can uncover or facts we can claim, even with all of the best critical methods and scholarly pursuits in the world. The truth of the Bible is offered to us in a relationship with the one to whom it testifies, the one whom it reveals, the one it bears to us: the crucified and risen Christ. When we enter the portals of this inexhaustible mine, the priceless treasure of God's love finds, recovers, and claims us.

So we return, time and again, to this book, just as we come creeping back to the font, in order to come face to face with our own deepest thirst and our inability to secure the drink we most need. We come to be drowned in its flood, washed in its mercy, and refreshed by its grace, until these words, this language is knit into our bones and we become living letters, bearers of the Word to others, for the sake of the life of the world.

Endnotes

[1] Martin Luther, "Preface to the Old Testament" in *Word and Sacrament I*, Luther's Works, vol. 35 (Philadelphia: Muhlenberg Press, 1960), 236.

[2] *The Adventures of Huckleberry Finn*, Mark Twain, (Scholastic, 1962), 2.

[3] *Moralia*, "Epistle" 4:177-78 [CCSL 143:6] as footnoted in Craig Koester's *Symbolism in the Fourth Gospel: Meaning, Mystery, Community*, second edition Minneapolis: Augsburg Fortress, 2003), 259. Gregory writes, "The Word of God . . . is, as it were, a kind of river, if I may so liken it, which is both shallow [*planus*] and deep, wherein both the lamb may find a footing, and the elephant float at large."

[4] Confession of Faith in the Constitution of the Evangelical Lutheran Church in America.

[5] Augustine, *The Confessions*, 1.16.26, Also translated "choice and precious vessels."

[6] Walter Bruggemann, *Genesis* (Louisville, Kentucky: John Knox, 1982), contents, ix.

[7] Eugene Peterson, *Tell It Slant: A Conversation on the Language of Jesus in his Stories and Prayers*, (Grand Rapids, Michigan: Wm. B. Eerdmans Publishing Co., 2008), 85-98.

[8] Helmut Thielicke, *The Waiting Father*, trans. John W. Doberstein (New York: Harper and Row, 1959).

[9] Kenneth E. Bailey, *The Cross and the Prodigal*. (St. Louis: Concordia Publishing House, 1973), 54-55.

10. Craig R. Koester, *Symbolism in the Fourth Gospel: Meaning, Mystery, Community*, second edition, (Minneapolis: Fortress Press, 2003), 259.

11. See R. Alan Culpepper, *Anatomy of the Fourth Gospel: A Study in Literary Design* (Philadelphia: Fortress Press, 1983), 15-49, for an analysis of the narrator, including his use of the term "whispering wizard" from Thomas Mann's *Der Zauberberg*

12. John 1:39; 1:46; 4:29.

13. R. Alan Culpepper, *Anatomy of the Fourth Gospel: A Study in Literary Design* (Philadelphia: Fortress Press, 1983), 232.

14. Raymond E. Brown, *The Anchor Bible*, John, volume 1, note 9 (Garden City, New York: Doubleday, 1966), 170.

15. Confession of Faith in the Constitution of the ELCA.

Communicating the Word in the Congregation

Margaret A. Krych
Lutheran Theological Seminary at Philadelphia

Hearing the Word of God

The Word of God is God's self-revelation, self-expression, self-impartation, which is a direct personal challenge to humanity in our history. The Word of God, as Gerhard Ebeling reminds us, is an event, a deed, an act—the Hebrew word *dabar* is happening word.[1] When God speaks, things happen—a world is created, order is established, redemption is accomplished.[2]

The primary way in which God has spoken to us is in Jesus Christ. So Jesus Christ is properly called the Word of God, the Word incarnate. With the Gospel of John we understand Jesus Christ to be the enfleshed Word of God (John 1:14).

The opening article of the Augsburg Confession refers to the Word and the Spirit as members of God the Trinity.[3] And in [the Latin text of] Article III, the Word is referred to as the Son of God.[4] Thus, any claim to be, or to represent, the Word of God must be measured against Jesus Christ as the ultimate Word.

Hearing the Word, then, means hearing Christ.

Because Christ is the incarnate Word of God, we also refer to the message *about* Christ as the Word. We call this message the gospel, since it is the good news of God's mercy and love shown in Christ for the forgiveness of sin by grace through faith. But the Word is not only good news. It is also serious news about our human situation—news of

God's judgment upon, and condemnation of, sin. So the Word is simultaneously a Word of judgment and mercy, of killing and making alive, of condemnation and salvation. In traditional Lutheran terms, the Word is both Law and Gospel.

The Bible has its center in the gospel, the good news of salvation in Jesus Christ. The definitive written witness to the Word in Christ is the Bible. The Bible in fact does something to us as we read it and hear it. It rebukes us, shows us our situation before God. And, it brings us God's promises of salvation and forgiveness of sin. That is, it speaks the word of law and gospel to us. Because the Bible is centered in this Word of law and gospel, we also use the term, "Word of God" for the Bible.[5] Through the Scriptures the Spirit speaks the Word of God to us and calls forth faith in us.[6]

For Luther, the Scriptures are "the loftiest and noblest of holy things, as the richest of mines which can never be sufficiently explored."[7] Luther says, "It is in Scripture and nowhere else that he [Christ] permits himself to be found"[8]—the Scriptures are the swaddling clothes and the cradle of Christ.[9]

The Word of God comes to us not only in the Bible but also in preaching, in sacraments, in the word of absolution, and as Christians speak the gospel one-on-one to each other. In these ways, the Word comes to us today.

Teaching the Bible in the Parish and Beyond

We will look at six questions to highlight requirements for teaching the Bible so that the Word might be heard today.

1. What means of interpretation (hermeneutics) is helpful in teaching the Bible?

Teaching the Bible must be grounded in an appropriate hermeneutic (means of interpretation). We have said that the Word is both Law and Gospel. Law and Gospel are the hermeneutical key to interpreting the Scripture. Law and Gospel must be distinguished and never confused. Yet the two are deeply interrelated. By revealing to us our sin the law drives us to the gospel message. Unless learners first perceive through the law their true state before God they will not hear the gospel. Yet there is also a real sense in which only when the gospel is known do we genuinely understand the law. Neither gospel nor law can be taught without the other.[10]

This means that whenever we approach the Scriptures, we must always ask, "What is the Word of God in this passage?" Or, more correctly, we should ask, "What is the Bible doing to me, to us, in this passage? In what way is this text law, a word of rebuke? How does this text judge us? How does it present God's demands of us? How does it drive us to our knees to ask for forgiveness? And, in what way is this text gospel? How does it tell us of a faithful God who loves and forgives in spite of who I am and what I have done? How does it remind us of God's promises and mercy in Christ?"

At any one time the text might either convict of sin or comfort us with the assurance of God's mercy—or both. The same words might be experienced by one learner as law and by another as gospel; or, a learner may hear a text on one occasion as accusing and on another occasion as comforting. And this is true of both Old and New Testaments.

When we read the Scriptures, it is the message of salvation which is at stake. The Word and justification by grace through faith are integrally related. Melanchthon writes that one cannot deal with God or grasp him except through the Word.[11] Therefore justification takes place through the Word. In the Large Catechism, Luther says, "In order that this treasure might not be buried but be put to use and enjoyed, God has caused the Word to be published and proclaimed, in which he has given the Holy Spirit to offer and apply to us this treasure, this redemption."[12]

In teaching, then, we shall attempt to interpret the Bible so that the Word will speak to the students in the very life situations in which they find themselves day by day. We shall then not teach Bible facts for the sake of filling the learner full of information, but rather for the purpose of communicating the good news of God's love and mercy proclaimed for the student. We will ask: What is the central meaning of the narratives? Why did the authors incorporate them into these books? What are they trying to say? What might they have said long ago? And—most important—what might they be saying today, to the church, and to me?

Today, Law and Gospel are not terms that people use in the supermarket or the college student center. Fifty years ago, theologian Paul Tillich argued for using more everyday words to describe the same realities; he suggested "questions" and "answers." He built his entire three-volume systematic theology around the Reformation understanding of law as that which reveals to human beings our sinful state and thus drives us toward, opens us up to the need of, the gospel, the promise of the forgiveness of sin for Christ's sake. And, Tillich started all preaching and teaching with an analysis of the human situation to expose the deep questions, existential questions, that are true of all of us. He used many disciplines to illustrate the human condition of sin, with its conflicts, anxiety, estrangement, and ambiguity. Then he correlated the answers of the gospel with those questions to show how God's revelation brings healing and acceptance and wholeness and peace to our human situation. The content or substance of the answer to our needs can never be derived from our human situation; the answer comes solely from God's revelation; it is inevitably spoken *to* our existence from beyond it.[13]

Whether we use the traditional terminology of Law and Gospel or something more common such as question and answer, or even different terminology that gets at the same thing, our concern in teaching is so to communicate the gospel that the learner is brought to faith by the Holy Spirit. Any communication of biblical knowledge must affect our students' existence, their very being.[14] While Law and Gospel may be familiar terms to many professionals, to persons in the pew they may be very foreign. Seminary students (who may be considered very dedicated lay persons, or they would not have given up their previous careers to come to seminary) are often totally unfamiliar with the idea of listening to what the Bible is saying in these terms when they first come to seminary. They find the idea that the Bible does something to them to be a very new notion. And, they often erroneously assume that the Old Testament is all law and the New Testament is all gospel. They need help in listening to the Scriptures and understanding that texts from both testaments can speak a Word of law or of gospel. I suspect this is true of the vast majority of our adult laity in parishes.

If we teach with a law-gospel approach, we may begin a class session with the biblical text to elucidate both question and answer. Or, the teacher may begin with the human question as experienced by the learner today[15] and then move to the biblical text. In either case, we must take seriously both the biblical text and the learner's life situation.

Of course, the way that students experience question and answer, or Law and Gospel, will differ depending on their circumstances and background. Teaching the Bible means participating in the life-situations of our students in such a way that we can appreciate how they will experience God's rebuke and God's mercy.[16] We need to understand and experience the culture or subculture of which the learner is a member in order to express the human question and the gospel answer in ways meaningful to the learner.[17] This is true of teachers working with the world of children, of teachers in our pluralistic society working with persons of different ethnic or regional backgrounds than their own, and of teachers dealing with members of the youth subculture. We need to take the time and effort to understand and appreciate the student's situation in a way that will enable the clear communication of the biblical message.

Teaching the Bible prepares learners for receiving the Word today through preaching and sacraments. In preaching, the biblical texts speak to us anew, rebuking us and bringing us God's promise of forgiveness, calling for our response of faith. Studying the Scriptures arises out of our baptism and should be a daily reminder of that proclamation of God's forgiveness of sins, of our dying and rising with Christ. The sharing of the holy supper is a proclamation of the Word and drives us back to the Scriptures. For the believer, worship and daily living are deeply inter-related with study of the Scriptures. And teaching the Bible also prepares the learners to speak the gospel to others in their everyday life situations.

2. What age-level appropriate concerns should be kept in mind when teaching the Bible?

Teaching the Bible must be done in a way that is appropriate to the age-level. Too often we have tried to teach children the same biblical content as youth and adults. And, we have supposed that if persons learn enough in childhood—or at least through early adolescence and the rite of Affirmation of Baptism—then they have pretty well learned all they need for life. But, research in cognitive development in the latter half of the twentieth century up through today shows us that this assumption is dead wrong. We now know that children think qualitatively differently from adults. Their brain cells and thus their thinking develop through stages—three stages before the age of two, a preoperational stage from two to seven years, a concrete thinking stage from around seven to twelve-plus years, and the final stage of abstract thinking that continues through adult life.[18]

The Bible was written by adults for adults. It presupposes abstract thinking on the part of the reader/hearer. Therefore a very large part—some would say most—of the Bible is not suitable for teaching to children younger than twelve-and-one-half years of age. So, we have the huge task of teaching probably most of the Bible to youth and adults. Actually, the task is even more complicated. It turns out that children are not sponges, taking in what is taught and letting it lie there until they are old enough to understand it. Rather, they interpret what they learn in terms of the way they are able to think at the time they are taught. This means that they misinterpret what is taught at too young an age—that is, before they are ready to grasp its true meaning. So, when we attempt to teach youth and adults, we often need to help them first unlearn what they have already misinterpreted and then help them explore the meaning of the biblical passages. Youth and adults may have misconceptions they have carried for years. Parables, for example, require abstract thinking that can appreciate metaphor. Before age twelve, most children take parables literally. The parable of the lost coin, taken literally, means that we should search for lost money or lost valuables. The young child who cannot deal with analogy or metaphor misses the "secret" or hidden meaning of God seeking those lost in sin. A child will naturally act out the role of God instead of the role of the coin. Parables are best taught after the age of twelve years when the abstract thinker can grasp metaphor. But, by then many teenagers dismiss them as "stories I heard as a little kid," and the motivation for reflecting on the story is low.

When we teach the Bible to children we should carefully select appropriate passages that they are able to appreciate in concrete and literal terms. There are many such passages—stories of friends such as David and Jonathan, and Jesus and his disciples; stories of families; stories of God helping people do difficult tasks; and for older children, stories of heroes who loved God; and so on. Plenty of wonderful passages!

Teaching biblically will mean communicating the good news, the *kerygma*, in the passage. So, instead of telling a parable, it may be more helpful to say directly to the young child, "Even when we do things that are not what God wants us to do, and even when we are the kind of people God doesn't want us to be, God still goes on loving us. God is like that all the time."

It is not until nine or ten years of age that children can appreciate historical contexts, different cultures, and multiple authors; not until adolescence can they deal with intricate editing details and the way in which stories functioned in the early church. All these points are essential to understanding many Bible passages.

Faculty members are well aware that we have students entering college who really need to learn how to read the Bible. And students enter seminary either confessing that they have little Bible background, or alternatively, imagining they know the Bible and then they have a faith crisis in the first year because they feel the course professors "took away Jesus and the Bible" as they have known them. And, in the parish, we have adults too proud or too ashamed to admit that they misunderstand many Bible passages; so to avoid embarrassment they avoid Bible study altogether—or they prefer large anonymous forums where they can listen but not ask questions or be challenged. And much of this situation has arisen because we have taught too much too soon to children and not enough to teenagers and adults. In a recent study, while the numbers of congregations having Sunday school and Bible studies is laudable, the actual number of adult participants leaves a great deal to be desired.[19]

So, much of what I will focus on here will be directed to older adolescent and adult learning, because that is where there is a serious void in teaching the Bible in the parish and beyond.

Historically, Christian education was first for adults who were converted to the faith. Only after Constantine approved Christianity in the fourth century did the church take children's education seriously and then within the context of the family. Even Luther folded children's education into teaching in the home, although he also pleaded for schools to engage in the task as well. In planning home education, Luther was savvy—he included adult education, with adults learning so that they could teach the children and servants in the household. Luther wanted all adults to learn throughout their lives,[20] and we should expect no less.

In teaching, we seek the help of biblical scholars in ascertaining the "authentic" meaning of a passage, and then we make the judgment at which age that meaning is most appropriately taught to children or youth or adults. We need to avoid teaching material that is beyond the child, and we also need to avoid watering down the meaning of the passage so that it is "suitable"—a prime example being the session for kindergarten students in which the feeding of the five thousand was presented as a story about "Jesus, the man who loved outdoor picnics"! Incidentally, those who produce children's Bibles often do not select stories on the basis of cognitive development. Instead, they choose stories that adults will buy because adults love them—without regard to whether children can understand them or even might be frightened by them.[21]

Children need to hear the gospel in terms that reach them at their stage of development. They do not have to learn the whole Bible in childhood. The study of the Scriptures is for a lifetime, and there are many passages that are best learned in the teenage or adult years.

3. How will we use the Bible in class settings?

Good teaching uses the Bible joyfully and explicitly in the classroom. But, this has not always been the case in congregations, partly due to the fact that Christian education tends to follow trends or fads. In the 1960s and 1970s serious biblical content tended to give way to sharing of feelings and small group life. In the 70s and 80s we let adults choose topics that interested them—and many chose topics that were not biblical. We had courses in the arts and sociology and life transitions—all useful, but not necessarily geared to producing biblically literate adults. Of course, there were notable exceptions, such as the program "Word and Witness." In the 80s and 90s there was more cry for "Bible and theological basics" among professional Christian educators.[22] But, although heeded by some congregations, that demand did not translate into large numbers of congregations offering a good variety of biblical courses for adults and teenagers, nor did it result in large numbers of participants flocking to the courses that were offered. Today we hope that the Book of Faith Initiative in the ELCA might turn the tide and be the catalyst in 2010 and beyond that will bring about increased emphasis on solid biblical content for study in the parish and beyond.

It is time to reclaim for all members the sense that the Bible is the book of the church and the book of every Christian. It is our heritage, our mother-tongue.[23] We should read it joyfully and often, and study it as our right and responsibility as well as a privilege. Teaching the Bible means helping students rejoice in this heritage; welcoming their questions; seeking answers with them; and helping them formulate the most useful question: How can I hear God's Word in this passage?

In teaching, we need to preserve the authority of the Scriptures, a basic tenet of the Reformation. As the record of the apostolic witness to Christ, Scripture offers all that is necessary to salvation, and the church must measure all that it does and says by this authority. This normative role of Scripture can and should apply to curriculum development as well as to our own teaching, and should be the standard against which students measure their own theological understanding.

The way in which the Bible is handled in class can contribute to a good or a bad sense of what the Bible is about. The teacher who, because the copy of the Bible is expensive, says quickly, "Don't touch the Holy Bible with dirty fingers; don't write in the margins; don't drop it on the floor," may be communicating a bibliolatry that will last a lifetime. Let students treat the Bible like other books—if all books should be treated with respect, then put the treatment of copies of the Bible in that framework. Many have found that writing in the margin, underlining, and generally "making one's copy of the Bible one's own" can be very helpful for children as well as for youth and adults.

We must teach the Scriptures honestly. Gradually we can help elementary children and youth learn how various writings in the Bible may have developed. Very early in the elementary years children can understand that the gospel writers could not have written down every single thing that Jesus ever did, and so the writers chose the stories they considered most helpful for everyone to hear so that people would learn about Jesus and trust in him. Children can learn that the Bible is a special book because of what it tells us about God and God's love shown for us and for all people in Jesus Christ. They should be told clearly that the stories they learn in class are written in the Bible, and some day they will read them for themselves. Older elementary-age children can understand that various reports may describe an event differently. So these students can also appreciate different versions in the gospels of stories about Jesus. By the beginning of the abstract thinking stage in early adolescence students are ready to deal with different forms of literature in the Scriptures, and with sources and strands of tradition that have been incorporated into the biblical narrative.

Learners of all ages should not be shielded from the fact that the Bible contains historical, scientific, and even grammatical errors and discrepancies. Do not pretend that the Bible has no inconsistencies even to the younger children; such pretense will mean that when the child gets older she will feel betrayed because she has heard from you a dishonest word. Some passages are very difficult to understand, and even experts disagree on their meaning. As teachers, we need to be admit when we are puzzled and do not know the answer. If possible, we can promise to try to find an answer and report back to the class.

Above all, help students listen to what a passage has to say about God and God's gracious love and activity. Help them appreciate how ancient scholars loved the message and wanted to pass it on. Teach the Bible in such a way that your students will also love the message and want to pass it on. Teach them in a way that they will be drawn always to Christ.

4. What teaching methods are helpful in teaching the Bible?

Good teaching uses a variety of appropriate methods. In choosing any method, remember that the method itself communicates content. Unless content and method are congruent, the message we teach may actually be opposed to the official content. In other words, what we do must be consistent with what we say. If a teacher attempts to communicate the good news of God's unconditional acceptance of us in spite of our sinfulness, but then does not herself accept students in spite of who they are or what they do, then the students are likely to learn of rejection rather than of God's love.

Some methods are particularly helpful in teaching the Bible. Hearing Law and Gospel, for example, may best be done in small groups or by oneself. Small groups have an intimacy that allows persons to say what the text is doing to them—how they experience rebuke or promise. And, what may be rebuke for the teacher may be promise to the learner. So, each person should have opportunity to say how the passage deals with him or her.

Independent learning—learning done by an individual—is excellent because persons can learn at their own pace and can hear the gospel answer in terms that make sense to them. Independent learning may be preferred by those with busy schedules such as young adults and adults with families. A good library for children, youth, and adults is important in helping all age levels learn the Scriptures. It can be used by individuals, but also by classes and groups. It may take several years to build a good church library. You can use memorial money to get started with books dedicated in memory of loved ones. A good congregational library includes sets of commentaries at three levels—basic, intermediate, and advanced—and also includes concordances, Bible atlases, and Bible dictionaries. Quality is essential. Be sure books are accurate and up-to-date for all age levels, including those for children. And let children, youth, and adults know that the pastor and other teachers are readily available to help them wrestle with the meaning of biblical texts, not only during class time but also at other times and by email and by phone.

In teaching the Bible, as in all teaching, use methods that require participants to be active. Lectures are acceptable for large classes if participants actively take notes, but are not helpful if participants sit passively, and the lecture goes in one ear and out the other. Retention is about ten percent for passive listening and twenty percent for listening and seeing, but jumps to about eighty percent if students take notes, review, and then express their learning in some active way. You probably will not want to use exams or tests in the parish, but you can certainly take advantage of the fact that one of the best ways to retain learning is for the learners to then teach what they have learned to others.

Discussions also require active participation by group members. Discussion becomes problematic when persons fail to share insights or engage in critical reflection with others. Discussion is good for changing attitudes, but not good for learning information, unless there is an expert present or you use a printed or media resource to give informed input to the group.

Engage participants in active learning by asking them to prepare verbal or written or video or other media presentations on the Bible that they then share with the group. Or, have the group write its own biblical drama, design sets and costumes, and present the play to another group or to the whole congregation; this will result in learning for performers and for those who watch.

Include class techniques that are fun. Learning the Bible should be joyous, not drudgery! Try some games such as biblical versions of popular television quiz shows. For review of material, design your own biblical crossword puzzles or Bible word games, or download them free from the internet. Role-play biblical stories—there is adventure, pathos, victory, and comedy aplenty in the Scriptures. You might have participants write some songs or ballads about biblical characters or stories. Or, have a debate between two biblical characters.

Engage students in research by supplying resources in several centers in the classroom, with direction sheets to guide them in use of the materials. Participants can present their findings to the whole class. Elementary children as well as youth and adults learn well this way.

Cooperative procedures are effective. Students might work together in pairs or threes or small work groups to do a project. Think-pair-share has each person reflect on a biblical topic, then form pairs to discuss their reflections, and then share their findings with the class. Or, you can do a jigsaw project in which each member of the group completes research on a particular aspect of a biblical topic, then all members share their work with the others, and the group joins all the pieces together to form a finished Bible project.

Use technology in teaching. Always consider first whether a particular form of technology helps or hinders learning. For example, PowerPoint can be helpful in presenting diagrams and pictures and highlighting headings. But if the slides simply repeat detailed content that you present orally, PowerPoint may encourage passivity and thus hinder learning, especially if participants know they will get a handout of the slides at the end of the session. Another problem in using technology is that not all internet biblical websites have accurate information; so before teaching, consult biblical experts at colleges or seminaries for sites that may be trusted.

Locally, you might use wikis.[24] A wiki allows multiple users to write and edit a web document using wikispaces.com or other software. The value is that students will do research on a Bible topic, and others will add and edit the material as they do their research. The danger is that participants may share inaccurate information, so someone has to monitor the wiki. You also need to be sure that all participants understand copyright laws and acknowledge the sources of any ideas they use.

Or, you could develop your own Bible study and upload it to your church website. Time consuming, yes—but you can use a Bible study for several years by updating it regularly. The effort is worth your while because you can reach just about all members of the congregation. And, of course, you increase your own learning as you develop the study for others.

Or, you might use a blog to share insights on daily Bible readings with teenagers. Consider developing resources that congregational members can download on computers or mobile devices.

Some seminaries have biblical courses online for lay people. These give opportunity for serious biblical learning. Nowadays, some universities are beginning to put courses on their websites that can be downloaded at no cost. As this trend continues, look for the addition of courses from departments of religious studies.

5. What published resources can we use when teaching the Bible?

Teaching the Bible requires quality published resources. "Published" today means two kinds of resources—print and non-print. Printed resources are those that we have used for many decades. They usually come with a teacher guide, student book, and sometimes teacher resources. Or, for adults, there may be only one book that is used both by the leader and the students. Printed materials are relatively easy to use. They may or may not offer alternative methods to use in sessions—usually not many choices will be offered, because space is limited.

Exciting is the fact that we now also have non-print resources. Particularly for children and youth, we can go on-line and download course materials from church publishers. Because there is much less limit on space, such materials often give many alternative procedures so that you can actually build lesson plans with your own particular students in mind. Clearly this takes time—time that some teachers will not want to spend. And, you will pay for more printer cartridges on your home printer. Also, of course, there are congregations where not every teacher has a computer or wants to use it in this way.

Because of background, opportunity, and inclination adults need resources at several levels of learning—basic, intermediate, and advanced. Publishers vary on how many of each they publish. Unfortunately, they often overload on the light or basic level and have too few advanced level resources. Lay persons whose daily occupations call for them to apply deep thinking capacities may hit a wall in the church when they discover that there are not sufficient courses that really challenge them. It is, unfortunately, a vicious cycle. Until more adults get involved in learning and progress to an advanced stage, it is difficult for publishers to break even on resources that are used by few congregations.

Fortunately, publishers are becoming flexible. Materials for small buying groups can be produced less inexpensively as downloadable resources. Some books are able to be ordered on a print-on-demand basis.

Church publishing houses are sharing many more resources produced by congregations or synods. But, there is a long way to go. For example, there are too few resources in languages other than English, although the number has been slowly but steadily growing.

We also need curriculum that is balanced. Biblical expert Walter Brueggemann[25] suggests that we need a balance with three components—first, courses that set forth the "normative articulations of the faith" that "are not individual, private conjurings"[26]—the meat and potatoes of theology; second, prophetic courses that challenge the consensus and criticize that which has not been questioned;[27] and third, courses that focus on discernment, daily experience, and the interconnectedness of life[28] and in so doing celebrate human freedom and responsibility.

6. What trained leadership is critical for teaching the Bible in the parish (and beyond)?

Teaching the Bible requires trained leadership in the parish, college, seminary, and wider church. Trained professional leaders are God's good gift to the church for biblical teaching in the parish and beyond.

At the local level, parish pastors are called to teach Bible courses regularly—and at varied times in the day and on various days of the week that will suit the busy schedules of their members. In addition, it is helpful if pastors show interest by dropping in on classes taught by lay adults. Teachers say they drop out if no one stops by to show interest in the classes they teach.

Pastors need lifelong learning as much as everyone else. The church needs pastors who continue studies in both Bible and Christian education. Such advanced degree programs as master of sacred theology and doctor of ministry are great opportunities for pastors to develop Bible studies and to hone their teaching and organizational skills for parish ministry or chaplaincy work.

In church institutions, college professors of religion need to show love for the Scriptures they are teaching. Students can start their own groups on campus but may need guidance on choosing resources—and we can be thankful that there are good young adult materials such as those produced by the ELCA publishing house.

At seminaries, the Bible should be a loved book, not just for study but for hearing law and gospel daily by both faculty members and students. The danger in studying anything professionally is that the very study can extinguish real love and personal excitement for the material. Bible professors have a particular responsibility to keep the love and excitement burning brightly in their students.

Writers and professors in the fields of biblical studies and Christian education can and should have a mutually beneficial relationship. The one gives extremely important content for teaching and scholarly tools with which to appreciate and understand the scriptural text. The other can provide clear means of communicating the content as well as seeking in biblical theology grounding for its task and approach. More, and more thorough, courses in Christian education should be required in seminaries along with required biblical expertise. And, professional parish religious educators need good seminary training with formal preparation in biblical studies so they are adequate to the task of teaching the Bible. Biblical languages can be of great help to Christian educators. Sadly, some religious educators pursuing seminary degrees elect not to study Greek and Hebrew.

What we have said of the professional religious educator may also be said of many serious volunteer teachers in the congregation. Biblical scholarship and even languages (at least at a rudimentary level that will help in using scholarly commentaries) can be of tremendous help to the volunteer lay teacher. In fact, some lay people are better equipped than clergy to deal with languages, yet oddly we may hesitate to give them Greek lexicons or apologize for introducing linguistic points.

We need more training opportunities in teaching techniques. There are often workshops and training courses for those teaching children. But, fewer opportunities have been available to teachers of adults. We need more training courses and workshops for professionals and volunteers who seek to teach the Bible with adults. And we need persons who can act as consultants to teachers of all age levels in the parish and beyond. Synodical staff can be a blessing to the church in spearheading such opportunities. So can national staff.

Which brings me to say a serious word concerning staffing in the wider church. Cuts in personnel over the years since the inception of the

ELCA in 1988 have resulted in a serious lack of resource persons in the field of Christian education on the national churchwide staff. We believe that the Book of Faith Initiative is central to our current mission as a church. And we have said that: "In our time it is particularly important to renew in this church a culture of engagement with Scripture, catechesis and theological reflection that increases general biblical fluency and the capacity of all the baptized to understand their lives, the world, and the mission of the church through shared exploration of faith's wisdom."[29] If we are serious, we will mourn the cutting of national staff in the area of Christian education—staff who could help equip church colleges, church schools, synods, regional resource centers, youth networks, and congregations. "From the time of the Reformation, the Lutheran church has been a teaching and learning church."[30] The Bible has been at the heart of our teaching and learning. While understanding the need for cutting costs, we nevertheless should hope that the church may be able to reinstate churchwide staff positions that have responsibilities for children, youth, and adult educational ministries.

For the teaching of the Bible to be done well in parishes, all three levels—local, synodical, and national—must have the trained staff needed to ensure that teaching in parishes is of good quality and feeds the needs of the people. A lack at one level impoverishes the whole church.

Conclusion

We have looked at six questions. We have described six components that are necessary for good teaching of the Bible in the parish and beyond. But, ultimately, we teach knowing that it is the Holy Spirit who makes the Word effective and who, through the Word, calls forth faith in both teachers and students. Let us pray for the power of the Spirit in the serious teaching of children, youth, and adults so that the gospel might be heard, the faith of the people might be nurtured, and that laity might speak the Word to one another and learn of its implications for daily ministry. Let us pray for the success of the Book of Faith Initiative as a vehicle for persons to hear the good news of God's promises in Jesus Christ and to respond in faith. And, let us thank God for all who teach the Bible faithfully in the parish (and beyond). May they serve the church well.

Endnotes

1. Gerhard Ebeling, "Word of God and Hermeneutics" in *Word and Faith*, tr. James W. Leitch (London: SCM, 1963), 326. This description of the Word is similarly expressed in Margaret Krych, "The Gospel Calls Us" in Rebecca Grothe, ed., *Lifelong Learning* (Minneapolis: Augsburg Fortress, 1997), 24.

2. *Ibid.* (Krych)

3. It rejects all heresies which deny the divinity of the Word.

4. *The Book of Concord*, ed. Robert Kolb and Timothy Wengert (Minneapolis: Augsburg Fortress, 2000), 36-37.

5. Margaret Krych, *The Ministry of Children's Education: Foundations, Contexts and Practices* (Minneapolis: Fortress Press, 2004), 21.

6. See, Krych "The Gospel" in Grothe, *Lifelong Learning*, 24-25.

7. Martin Luther, "Prefaces to the Old Testament," *Luther's Works*, Vol. 35 (Philadelphia: Muhlenberg Press, 1960), 236.

8. Martin Luther, Sermon on "The Gospel for the Festival of the Epiphany," *Luther's Works*, Vol. 52, 171.

9. *Ibid.*

10. Margaret Krych, *Teaching the Gospel Today* (Minneapolis: Augsburg, 1987), 26.

11. Melanchthon, Apology of the Augsburg Confession, *Book of Concord*, 131:67.

12. Luther, Large Catechism, *The Book of Concord*, 436: 38.

13. Paul Tillich, *Systematic Theology*, Vol. 1 (Chicago: University of Chicago Press, 1951), 1-68. Also see Margaret Krych, *Teaching the Gospel Today*, chapter 2, and *The Ministry of Children's Education*, 7.

14. Such existential knowledge Tillich termed "uniting or receiving knowledge." *Systematic Theology*, Vol. 1:98. Rudolf Bultmann saw that what was crucial was not the world view of the first century and the mythological framework in which the *kerygma* was couched, but rather the central message itself that addresses us personally at the very center of our existence. *Jesus Christ and Mythology* (London: SCM, 1958), 14-18, 40, 53, 63, 66-70. ". . . To hear the Scriptures as the word of God means to hear them as a word which is addressed to me, as *kerygma*, as a proclamation. Then my understanding is not a neutral one, but rather my response to a call." *Ibid.*, 71.

15. In the latter case, Tillich himself suggested that the teacher's role is to help the learners become aware of the questions which they already have and then to show how the biblical answers correlate with precisely those questions. In addition, it is the task of the teacher to help learners develop the capacity to formulate the deepest human questions to which the gospel is answer. Paul Tillich, *Theology of Culture* (New York: Oxford University Press, 1964), 206.

16 Tillich emphasized the importance of the teacher's "participation" in the situation of the learner. (*Ibid.*, 205)

17 "Participation means participation in their existence out of which the questions come to which we are supposed to give the answer." *Ibid.*

18 See Krych, *The Ministry of Children's Education*, 8-9.

19 In the 2008 Faith Communities Today Survey of ELCA Congregations (a sample of 603 ELCA Congregations as part of the FACT study) 93 percent reported having Sunday church school and 92 percent reported Bible studies in addition to Sunday church school. But, only 35 percent described their congregations as having serious study of Scripture and theology (http:lrc.elca.org, accessed 8/24/10). Comparisons of the 2001 survey with the 2008 survey show that attendance has been relatively stable in Christian education in the last decade with 23.7 percent checking that they were active in Sunday church school and 23.7 percent checking active in Bible study. However, since the survey participants could check both categories, this may mean that only about one quarter of adults are regularly engaged in learning in parishes. (U.S. Congregational Life Survey, Frequencies for ELCA Attendees, 2001 and 2008, from Research and Evaluation, ELCA)

20 Luther considered the catechism "the minimum of knowledge required of a Christian." "Anyone who does not know it should not be numbered among Christians nor admitted to any sacrament," he says (Preface to the Large Catechism, The Book of Concord, 383:2). Nor does Luther consider the Small Catechism to be sufficient. In the preface to the Small Catechism (*The Book of Concord*, 349:17) he urges those responsible, after they have taught the Small Catechism, to "then take up a longer catechism and impart to them a richer and fuller understanding." For those who could not grasp more, the very basics of the catechism were acceptable. But Luther expected most baptized persons first to learn the parts of the catechism, then to be instructed in their meaning, and then to study a large catechism.

21 There are some pretty scary stories in the Bible—Joseph's brothers drop him in a pit, Daniel gets thrown into a lion's den because he prays, Samuel's mother drops him off at the temple and leaves him there, and only Noah with a small number of animals and family members is saved while God drowns all the rest of the children and babies and mommies and daddies in a huge rain storm.

22 For a brief history of the movements in twentieth century Christian education, see Krych "The Gospel Today," in Grothe, *Lifelong Learning*, 14-15.

23 To borrow a phrase from Professor Karlfried Froelich of Princeton Theological Seminary, in a lecture at the Lutheran Theological Seminary at Philadelphia, 1995.

24 For this and other interesting methods, see Barbara Gross Davis, *Tools for Teaching*, 2nd ed. (San Francisco, Jossey-Bass, 2009), Part V.

25 Brueggemann builds his "balance" on the canon of the Old Testament that includes Torah, prophetic literature, and the Writings. See Walter Brueggemann, *The*

Creative Word: Canon as a Model for Biblical Education (Philadelphia: Fortress Press, 1982), passim.

26. *Ibid.*, 17.
27. *Ibid.*, 40-41.
28. *Ibid.*, 84-86.
29. From the Initial Summary Statement of the draft "For Discussion in Vocation and Educating Seminary Planning Circles" (10/15/2009), 1.
30. Our Calling in Education (social statement adopted at 2007 ELCA churchwide assembly), 13.

Enacted Utterances:
Tracing the Power of the Divine in Luke

Richard Carlson
Lutheran Theological Seminary at Gettysburg

This year, in conjunction with the ongoing emphasis on the Book of Faith, the presenters for the Hein-Fry lectures have been asked to take a bit of a different tack. Instead of talking about the Bible and how we interpret it, the presenters have been asked to focus more on teaching the Bible, particularly in parish settings, so that the Bible could be better interpreted and understood as God's written word speaking to contemporary lives. So in many and various ways, this presentation will very much overlap with what is regularly done in a Bible study.

If someone would ask, "What is the key for being able to teach the Bible effectively?" I would respond by saying the key is being able to read the Bible effectively. Establishing honed, outcome-oriented objectives for a Bible study are indispensible so that one knows what they are trying to do in and through a Bible study. Utilizing various learning-oriented methodologies for a Bible study are valuable tools for accomplishing such established objectives. Helping empower people to become fluent in the first language of faith, the Bible, is a fantastic vision for Bible study and biblical resources in our church today, particularly as they relate to the Book of Faith initiative. Nevertheless, all of these components are predicated and built upon a foundation of being able to read the Bible effectively.

People who are called leaders of the church have been trained to various degrees in reading the Bible effectively. Many have even been equipped with distinctive linguistic skills to read biblical texts in their original language. They know and even practice much of what is about to be presented. Still, it can always be helpful to stop for a moment and consider anew how we are doing what we are doing when it comes to reading the Bible effectively. Hence in that which follows, a broad model for reading the Bible will be introduced and then that model will be put to use in order to investigate a distinctive theological and narrative emphasis in Luke's gospel. In this way, both theory and practice will be employed in order to consider ways to read the Bible more effectively.

Reading the Bible effectively in many ways entails navigating one's way through three interrelated and yet distinctive worlds: the World of the Biblical Text, the World Behind the Biblical Text, and the World in Front of the Biblical Text, as the following model seeks to illustrate.

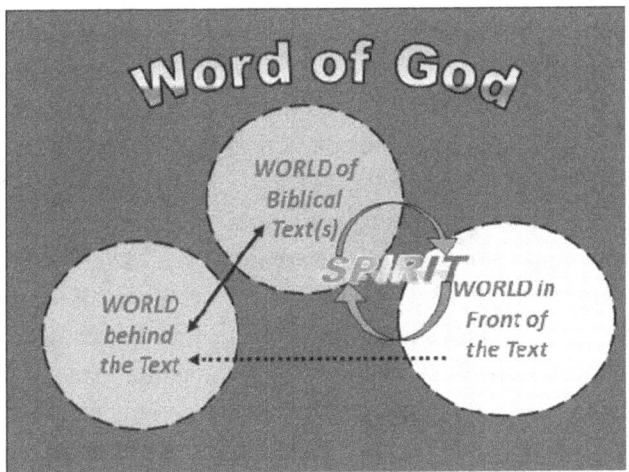

The World in Front of the Biblical Text is, in many ways, the easiest world to navigate because it includes the interpretive world in which we live, move, and have our being. But this world is also bigger than just our immediate ministerial and social contexts. This world includes

- Past readings of the text
- Contemporary church life, praxis, proclamation
- Church traditions and histories
- Confessional stances and theological perspectives
- Contemporary societal realities
- Reading communities, methods, strategies
- Various social, gendered, ethnic, age realities of readers, etc.

All of this, as well as additional contingencies, impact how the Bible is read and interpreted. Thus while contemporary Bible readers inhabit this World in Front of the Text, its sheer complexity of contingencies means that the Bible is going to be read in a myriad of ways by a myriad of readers, so that no one single reading will be regarded as the universally agreed upon reading of the text.[1]

The World Behind the Text involves the multifaceted dynamics of understanding ancient social structuring and interchanges (e.g., first century pre-industrial, agrarian society; honor/shame social values; patron/client social interchanges; etc.), construals of reality based on worldviews (e.g., patriarchy; concepts of purity; cosmology; etc.); political and historical realities related to the time when a given biblical work was constructed (e.g., imperial ethos, ideology, and propaganda; pre-70 CE, first-generation missional realities and post-70 CE second-generation ecclesiological realities; etc.);[2] and issues related to how the text came to be (e.g., source, form, redaction criticisms; transmission of traditions; dynamics related to various communities with their own particular theological and social realities; etc.). It is also important to note in the interpretive model at hand how there is a double arrow between the World Behind the Text and the World of the Text. That is, a host of factors in the World Behind the Text helped fashion and shape the World of the Text while at the same time the World of the Text regularly sought to address and at times even undermine the social, political, and religious realities and structures existing in the World Behind the Text.[3] The more that contemporary biblical readers/interpreters understand the World Behind the Text, the better they are able to read and interpret the World of the Biblical Text.

The World of the Biblical Text refers to a given book in the Bible. As regards Luke's gospel, for example, the World of the Biblical Text would involve the entire Gospel of Luke so that an investigation of a passage such as Luke 1:26-38 (what subsequently came to be called the annunciation in the World in Front of the Text) would need to consider not only these thirteen verses but where this particular text fits into and relates to the whole of the Lukan narrative. Likewise, if one works with the assumption that the Book of Acts is the second volume of a progressive plot by the same author, then potential theological and narrative aspects arising from Acts would also be considered as part of the World of the Text. Finally, the

Old Testament—which to Luke is the scriptures of Moses, the prophets, and the Psalms—is in some significant ways to be understood as part of the World of the Text because the author of Luke understands those scriptures to involve God's salvific promises which God is now fulfilling in the events being narrated in this two-volume story. Finally, this reading model operates with a confessional perspective that such an interpretive enterprise includes dynamic explorations guided and empowered by the Holy Spirit.[4] It is through the ongoing activity of the Holy Spirit that we are able to enter into the World of the Text and discover its contours and claims in order that the Word of God embedded in the World of the Text remains a living, dynamic Word in and for the World in Front of the Text. In this way, God's living, dynamic Word addresses us both individually and communally in the World in Front of the Text.[5]

As noted earlier, this year's Hein-Fry presenters have been asked to focus more on the realities of actually teaching the Bible, and so it is in this vein that the focus now shifts from discussing the broad contours of the interpretive model to investigating three particular and interrelated texts from Luke's gospel. These texts are Luke 1:5-38; 5:1-11; 24:1-12. As we enter into and explore the world of these three texts, we are also going to be mindful of the World Behind the Text which impacts the World of the Text and which the World of the Text at times seeks to subvert. Likewise we are going to seek to hear how the World of the Text is speaking to our lives in the World in Front of the Text as the Spirit works to challenge and sustain our lives and our missional commitments as individuals and as faith communities in the twenty-first century.

When one enters into the theological, narrative world of Luke 1:5-38, one is immediately introduced to topsy-turvy divine activity.[6] While the rest of our biblical investigation could be spent on these opening verses in Luke, here the focus is going to be on two key themes being established in these dual birth announcement scenes within the Lukan World of the Text. The first aspect is what scholar Joel Green has described as the topsy-turvy nature of divine activity. In the World Behind the Text, there are certain standards of judgment which would be expected to be made with regard to the comparisons and contrasts of the two key human characters, Zechariah and Mary. In the World Behind the Text, Zechariah has all the proper credentials, including the fact that he is:

- Male
- Old
- Priest
- Righteous
- Married to a righteous, female priestly descendant
- Chosen by God to officiate at the incense altar in the temple
- A father-to-be patterned after Abraham's experience

So based on the standards and evaluative judgments of the World Behind the Text, Zechariah would be regarded as having fairly high status and as being a reliable interpreter of divine activity.

Mary, however, has no apparent status or religious credentialing on her own because she is:
- Female
- Young
- Credentialed vis-a-via the man of Davidic descent to whom she is betrothed
- Stationary in the insignificant locale of Nazareth

She is not presented negatively, but with regards to her own inherent religious credentials or outward status, there is not much there. Consequently, she would not be expected to be much of a reliable interpreter of divine activity when utilizing the standards and criteria of the World Behind the Text.

Nevertheless, what does the World of the Text do to such standards or expectations from the World Behind the Text? It tips them completely upside down. This is particularly highlighted in the contrasting "knowing" questions each of the parents-to-be asks Gabriel on the heels of the divine birth announcements. Zechariah inquires about cognitive knowing when he asks, "According to what will I know [γνωσομαι/gnōsomai] this? For I myself am an old man, and my wife has become advanced in her years" (1:18). [8] How should Zechariah know that in God's plan an old man who is married to an old, barren woman can have a baby boy? Because this has happened before in God's designs! Abraham and Sarah, primer forbearers of the faith of Israel, had this same experience. If anyone should know that scriptural story it should have been Zechariah, the highly credentialed religious leader. But he has not remembered God's primary dealings with Israel, and so Zechariah asks the wrong knowing question.

Indeed, Gabriel marks such a question as unbelief on Zechariah's part so that (in an ironical angelic gesture) Zechariah's silence becomes his own way of knowing that Gabriel's birth utterance will be fulfilled in its own critical time, which will be in about nine months (1:19-22).

Mary, however, asks a very appropriate "knowing" question, "How will this be since I am not knowing [γνωσομαι/ginōskō] a man?" (1:34).[9] Her knowing question refers to basic human procreation in the World Behind the Text. Because she is not "knowing" a man (i.e., she is an engaged virgin who has not yet had sexual relations with a man), how can she possibly have a baby boy? That is impossible according to the ways and means of biology in the World Behind the Text. The answer to her question, however, involves God doing something incredibly new through the power of the Holy Spirit. Up to this point in the totality of the World of the Text stretching back to Adam and Eve, a woman who has not "known" a man has not become pregnant. Now, however, God's topsy-turvy activity in the World of the Text means that which is otherwise impossible becomes the stuff of divine possibility, and this non-statused teenage girl responds by opening herself up to such divine radical newness.

In connection to this, the second crucial aspect of this text which needs to be investigated involves the twice-used Greek word *rhēma* (ρημα). *Rhēma* is a delightful Greek word which can potentially have the interrelated meanings of "word" or "thing."[10] In this way, *rhēma* can refer to that which is spoken, or it can refer to an event or action, so that *rhēma* becomes its own double-entendre meaning "utterance" and/or "enactment." Here in the World of the Text the interrelated nature of both meanings of *rhēma* as utterance and/or enactment comes in the last two verses of our text. After explaining to Mary about the overshadowing power of the Holy Spirit and about Elizabeth's own pregnancy (1:35-36), Gabriel sums up divine activity by noting, "Because every *rhēma* is not impossible for God" (1:37). To this theological conclusion Mary immediately responds, "Look, the Lord's slave girl. Let it happen to me according to your *rhēma*" (1:38). The inherent polyvalence of *rhēma* is pregnant with meaning here (polyvalent pun intended). Is Gabriel claiming that every utterance is not impossible for God, or that every enactment is not impossible for God? Is Mary opening herself up to serve divine utterance or divine enactment? In the World of the Text, the answer is "Yes!" The absolutely crucial theological point being established here in the very opening of

Luke's story is that every divine *rhēma* is not impossible for God to enact. In other words, that which God speaks, God will enact.

Not only is this a prime theological dictum to be repeated throughout Luke's theological narrative, it remains a crucial aspect of divine activity in our lives in the World in Front of the Text.

- "God can't forgive my sins. They are too terrible."
- "We can't be expected to share what Jesus means to us with other people."
- "I can't afford to give my money. The economy is so bad."
- "That program will never work in our church."
- "It's all impossible."

Yet the Word embedded in the World of the Text which speaks to us in the World in Front of the Text continues to be that for God, every *rhēma* is not impossible. Thus through these contrasting birth announcements to would-be parents, the question for us becomes: Who is our model for the way we will respond to the divine *rhēma*? Is it to be Zechariah or Mary?[11]

The second passage from the world of Luke's text to be considered for its apparent impossible nonsense is the calling of the first disciples (Simon Peter and Zebedee's sons) in Luke 5:1-11. Up to this point in the flow of Luke's story, Jesus is carrying out his God-given gospel mission in his hometown of Nazareth (4:16-30) and elsewhere in both Galilee and Judaea (4:14-15, 31-44). Now Jesus is going to engage people with the Word of God from a boat at the edge of the lake of Gennesaret as throngs of people have crowded together to hear him (5:1). In the World of the Text, this is not the first time Simon Peter appears. A few verses prior to this the text tells how Jesus had entered Simon's house and healed Simon's mother-in-law from a high fever on a Sabbath day (4:38-39). So when Jesus engages Simon in this text, Simon knows about and has experienced Jesus' power as a healer.

In 5:2-5a there is a detail regarding the fishermen's activity which to those in the World in Front of the Text could seem a bit strange. The fishermen are washing their nets after an entire night's worth of fishing (5:2b,5a). It is potentially strange in that their nets have already been in the water throughout the night and yet they had not caught a single fish in those nets. So why are they bothering to wash their soggy, non-fish tainted nets? Here is where information from the World Behind the Text can help in understanding something that might not automatically make sense in the World in Front of the Text. New Testament scholar, Joel Green, indicates that these were most likely particular or distinctive type of nets called "trammel nets" which are "made of linen, visible to fish during the day and so used at night . . . and requiring washing each morning. . . . Normally during the day, fish would see and avoid the net."[12] So even though they had not caught any fish the previous night, the mesh linen of their nets would require cleaning, thus explaining the narrative detail that they were washing their nets.

Nevertheless the oddities within the text have not vanished. Consider, for example, Jesus' command that the fishermen put out into the deep water and let down their freshly washed nets. First, there is no indication that Jesus is a fisherman. Yet here he is, the amateur, telling professional fishermen how to do their job. Second, what did the professional fishermen not catch all night long? Fish. So what do they expect not to catch in the morning? Fish. And yet here is Jesus, the amateur, giving the professional fishermen a task which would seem to have absolutely no chance of succeeding. Third, Jesus wants them to use a net designed for night fishing during the daytime so that even the dumbest fish could see the net and hence avoid being caught. All the outward circumstances seem to mark this is an impossible utterance on Jesus' part. And yet, what has the World of the Text clearly established? Every utterance is not impossible with God.

Indeed, what is the only reason that Simon gives for going along with Jesus' bidding, even though they have labored all night long without catching squat? On the basis of Jesus' *rhēma*, as Simon responds, "Master after toiling throughout the night we got nothing. But by your *rhēma* I will let down the nets" (5:5b). Even though every instinct seems to be telling Simon that this is a useless action, he does it because of Jesus' utterance. While Simon may not fully understand the intricacies of divine *rhēma*, the alert readers in the World in Front of the Text have already been conditioned to expect not just the unexpected but the seemingly impossible when it comes to divine *rhēma*, because divine utterances quickly become divine enactments. Thus when Simon puts out to the deep water and lowers the nets because of Jesus' *rhēma*, what happens? The enactment of the utterance happens as they hit the mother lode of fish (5:6-7). They do not just catch some fish but catch so great a haul of fish that their nets are tearing; so great a haul of fish that they signal their partners in another boat to come and help; so great a haul of fish that when they land the fish in the boats, the boats themselves begin to sink.

Simon Peter's response to all of this continues the text's oddities. First, the boat is so fully of floppy fish that it is beginning to sink. But what does Simon Peter do when he is apparently knee deep in a boat brimming with floppy fish? He falls at Jesus' knees (5:8a). The imagery here is starkly comic. The boat is sinking. Fish are flopping all around Jesus' knees, and Simon Peter joins them by kneeling into the immense catch of floppy fish. Second, Simon Peter's response is a combination of nonsense and misdirected theology as he tells Jesus, "Go away from me because I myself am a sinful man, Lord." (5:8b) Where are Jesus and Simon Peter when he tells Jesus to depart from him? They are in the deep water of the lake. The nonsense is that he seems to expect Jesus to climb out of the boat and walk on the water all the way to the shore. The misdirected theology involves the reason he tells Jesus to depart. It is not because he is upset that Jesus is sinking their boats; it is not because he wants to lighten the load in hopes of keeping the boats afloat. It is because he perceives himself as a sinful person and Jesus as a revered figure who should not be associating with sinners. Yet Simon Peter's perception of Jesus is completely backwards. On the one hand, in the World of the Text Jesus' mission has already been introduced as one in which he brings release (4:18), and as the narrative continues to unfold such release expressly includes forgiveness of sins (24:47; Acts 2:38; 5:31; 10:43; 13:38; 26:18). On the other hand, Jesus' ongoing, intentional association with sinners and the forgiveness of their sins he regularly extends to them will regularly get him into trouble with religious authorities (5:17-32; 7:36-50; 15:1-32; also see 19:1-10). Thus Jesus has been sent to utter and enact divine salvation precisely to sinful people who are sinking in a boat of floppy fish.

Not only is a sinner such as Simon Peter the object of Jesus' saving mission, but he is also being called to participate in that same saving mission as Jesus informs Simon Peter: "From now on you will be continuously catching people" (5:10b). The response of Simon Peter and the sons of Zebedee again produces a bit of a narrative oddity as the text notes that after bringing the boats ashore they leave everything and follow him (5:11). Again, what is in their boats? Fish. How much fish? More fish than they have ever caught. They have struck it rich in fish. This is the mother lode of all fish catches for these professional fishermen! And what do they do? Leave it all behind. At least they might have sold the fish, collected their profits, and then followed Jesus. But no! Profits, possessions, and professions—all that stuff which normally defines persons' lives in the World Behind the Text—now do not determine their actions, their attitudes, their conduct. Now divine utterances and enactments flowing through Jesus are shockingly in control of human lives.

Not only is this true in the World of the Text, it remains just as true and relevant for us in the World in Front of the Text.

- Why do we dare baptize an infant, particularly if there are no real guarantees that the parents will actually fulfill the vows they are taking? Lord, the parents are not going to bring the child back to church.

- Why do we dare to think—to trust—that Jesus is really present in/with/under a small morsel of bread and nothing more than a mere sip of wine? Lord, it is just bread and wine.

- Why do we seek to go out of our way to welcome people into our gatherings; people whose skin, whose language, whose economic status, whose sexual orientation may be so vastly different from ours? Lord, we really do not feel comfortable having all those other people around us.

- Why do we have the audacity to share our money with a denomination whose future seems questionable amidst a cruddy economy and so much turmoil? Lord, the ELCA is on the skids. We should not throw good money after bad.

- Why waste our time spreading the gospel in an indifferent, post-Christian world in which our message seems as relevant to people's lives as a deodorant commercial? Lord, people in our world today do not care about coming to church one hour a week let alone believing our message or living a life of committed discipleship.

- Lord, we have been fishing all night and we have not caught a single thing—not even a cold. But because of your *rhēma* . . . Oh Lord, how did all these floppy fish suddenly get into our boat?

Beginning in the ninth chapter of Luke, about one third of the way through this gospel narrative, the World of the Text takes a new and radical turn as Jesus first announces and then embarks on his passion journey which is to unfold in Jerusalem (9:31,51,53). The dramatic turn opens with the first in a series of passion prophecies in which Jesus' now announces: "It is necessary that the son of humanity suffer many things and be rejected after testing by the elders and chief priests and scribes and be killed and on the third day be raised" (9:22). A short while later in this very same chapter (and just nine days later in the plot of the story) a second passion prophecy is uttered by Jesus to his disciples:

> "Put these words into your ears. For the son of humanity is about to be handed over into human hands." They kept not understand this *rhēma*. It had been continuously hidden from them in order that they would not understand it, and they kept being afraid to ask him about this *rhēma* (Luke 9:44-45).[13]

While this particular prophecy offers no new details regarding the impending passion itself, three new insights are presented here. First, Jesus' passion prophecy is described as a *rhēma*, thus recalling and drawing on what has already been established about how every *rhēma* is not impossible for God, and how humans are called upon to open themselves up to such divine *rhēma* (as did Mary, the shepherds, Simeon, and Simon Peter) even when it seems impossible to be enacted. Second, strangely enough, the disciples do not comprehend such *rhēma* because God has hidden it from them so that they would not understand it, at least not at this point in the story. Third, for some reason which is not immediately clear, this *rhēma* about Jesus' passion keeps causing the disciples to be afraid. Is it because they do not want to appear stupid? Is it because they fear Jesus' prophesied passion will become true? Is there something so foreign about the *rhēma* itself that it causes fear? The narrative does not provide a clear answer, but keeps it ambiguous at this point in the plot.

All of this creates a significant disconnect between the disciples as characters in the World of the Text and the readers in the World in Front of the Text. Alert readers have known from the beginning of the story that every *rhēma* is not impossible for God. They have been shown that what divine agents such as Gabriel or Jesus have uttered will most definitely be enacted. Hence readers in the World in Front of the Text can fully anticipate that the details of the passion will be enacted in the World of the Text because Jesus has now uttered them. Yet the disciples who are accompanying Jesus to that very passion are totally unable to comprehend that which Jesus has uttered. Hence how will they ever be able to comprehend their enactment?

This disconnect is reinforced through a subsequent scene in which Jesus again presents a passion prophecy, and the disciples are again prevented from understanding this *rhēma*.

> After taking aside the twelve he said to them, "Look! We are going up to Jerusalem, and all that has been written through the prophets about the son of humanity will be completed. For he will be handed over to the Gentiles; and he will be mocked and insulted and spat upon. After they have flogged him, they will kill him, and on the third day he will rise again." But they understood nothing about these things and this *rhēma* had been continuously concealed from them and they kept not knowing the things which were being said (18:31-34).[14]

Once again the disciples do not understand because this *rhēma* of Jesus is being intentionally concealed from them by the unseen divine hand. Thus the significant gap stands between comprehending the impending passion *rhēma* by the readers in the World in Front of the Text and the divine concealment of the impending *rhēma* with respect to the disciples in the World of the Text. The interpretive issue, then, does not involve what is going to happen to Jesus but what is going to happen to the disciples. That is, Jesus is going to journey to Jerusalem where he will be handed over, be rejected, be abused, be killed, and on the third day be raised precisely because this is the stuff of divine *rhēma* which will be enacted.[15] Instead, the issue involves how the disciples will come to comprehend the divine *rhēma*, especially given the fact that God is currently and intentionally concealing it from them.

In Luke 22–23, the gap grows ever wider as the readers in the World in Front of the Text observe two important aspects regarding the action in the World of the Text. First, everything which Jesus had prophesied is fulfilled in scene after scene.[16] Second, the disciples remain almost totally oblivious regarding such fulfillments to the point that they are no longer part of the action once sunrise on Friday arrives in 22:62. Thus the readers remain with Jesus in the midst of his suffering and death while the disciples do not.

Nevertheless, within this larger passion drama a potential solution to the dilemma of Jesus' incomprehensible and hidden passion *rhēma* is foreshadowed. In 22:33-34, Peter's impending three-fold denial was prophesied.

> And Peter said to him, "Lord with you I am prepared to journey even to prison and to death." Jesus said, "I say to you, Peter, a rooster will not crow today until three times you deny knowing me."

On the one hand, it is not at all surprising that Jesus' prophecy is fulfilled later that same evening when Peter does deny knowing Jesus three times (22:54-60a). What is surprising, however, is that Peter comes to realize that Jesus' prophecy has been fulfilled.

> At that moment, while Peter was still speaking, a rooster crowed. Upon turning the Lord looked intently at Peter, and Peter remembered the Lord's *rhēma*, how he had said to him, "Before the rooster crows today, you will deny me three times." And going out he wept bitterly (22:60b-62).

Here it would seem that comprehension is directly tied to remembering Jesus' *rhēma* after it has been enacted and then connecting the dots. That is, within the World of the Text it is impossible to comprehend Jesus' prophetic *rhēma* ahead of time, because God keeps this hidden until the enactment happens. But once the enactment occurs, characters are invited to remember Jesus' *rhēma* and so interpret things appropriately.

This new possibility for comprehension rooted in remembering Jesus' *rhēma* is exactly what unfolds in the opening scenes on the third day. In devotion to Jesus, the group of women who had served Jesus since the days of his ministry in Galilee and who had witnessed his death and burial (23:49-55) continue to serve Jesus even though he is now dead and buried in Jerusalem. After resting on the Sabbath, they come to cleanse Jesus' crucified corpse with spices and ointments they had prepared (23:56). Yet as the third day dawns and they arrive at the tomb, they immediately find what they do not expect to find, while at the same time they do not find what they had expected to find (24:1-3). They had not expected to find the stone rolled away from the tomb, but that is what they find. They had expected to find the corpse in the tomb, but that is exactly what they do not find. In the midst of the women's bewilderment, two men encounter them with a question and a command.

It happened while they were perplexed about this, and Look! Two men stood by them in dazzling apparel. While the women became frightened and hung their faces to the ground the two said to the women, "Why are you seeking the one who is living with the dead? He is not here. But he was raised. Remember how he spoke to you while he was still in Galilee saying that it was necessary that the son of human be handed over into the hands of sinful humans and be crucified and on the third day rise" (Luke 24:4-7).

Their question is rhetorical in that the women should not be seeking among the dead the one who is living. To understand why such seeking is not necessary involves the command to remember what Jesus had previously declared about the divine necessity of his being handed over, crucified, and rising.[17] It should also be noted that the two men do not try to prove anything about the resurrection to the frightened women. From the perspective of someone in the World in Front of the Text, neither they nor the women turn the tomb into a crime scene in which a CSI team can gather all the physical evidence in order to try and prove once for all that Jesus is no longer dead. Instead, the frightened women are commanded to remember that which Jesus had uttered about the divine necessity of his crucifixion and resurrection ahead of time.

The women elicit two interrelated responses. They remember Jesus' *rhēma*, and then they report Jesus' *rhēma*.[18]

> And they remembered his *rhēma*. When they returned from the tomb they reported all these utterances to the eleven and to all the rest. They were Mary Magdalene and Joanna and Mary the mother of James and the rest of the women with them. They were telling these utterances to the apostles (24:8-10).[19]

For those living in the World in Front of the Text, the key to Easter faith is the same as it is for these women in the World of the Text. Easter faith is not a matter of proofs or varying types of physical evidence. Rather it involves remembering Jesus' own *rhēma* regarding the divine necessity of his death and resurrection. At the very beginning of this theological narrative those in the World in Front of the Text discovered what Mary discovered as a character in the World of the Text: With God every *rhēma* will not be impossible. Now at the climax of the story Mary Magdalene,

Mary the mother of James, Joanna, and the rest of the women remember Jesus' *rhēma* and so go and tell how that which Jesus uttered regarding his death and resurrection has been enacted. Virgins do not get pregnant. Catchless fishermen do not use the wrong nets suddenly to catch so many fish that their boats are on the verge of sinking. Dead men neither tell no tales nor rise from the dead on the third day. These enactments do not happen and cannot possibly happen except when they are the divine enactments of that which has been divinely uttered. Easter faith in both worlds is not about proofs or physical evidence. Easter faith means that with God every *rhēma* is not impossible, especially when it comes to the resurrection of the dead.[20]

Ironically, the eleven apostles and the rest of the men evidently do not realize that every *rhēma* is not impossible for God and are not yet ready to emulate the women by remembering Jesus' passion *rhēma*.

> These *rhēma* appeared to be like BS in the apostles' view, and they kept not believing the women. After getting up, Peter ran to the tomb and stooping down he saw the linen clothes only, and he departed to his own place wondering about that which has happened (Luke 24:11-12).[21]

Here it is important to note that it is not the women's *rhēma* which seem like BS to the apostles and other men. Rather, it is Jesus' own *rhēma* that is eliciting such a visceral, negative response among them. To them, the divine necessity of Jesus' death and resurrection stands as "that which is totally devoid of meaning."[22] Consequently, these men remain unbelieving.[23] Should it surprise us, then, that in the World in Front of the Text many people emulate this same reaction as they too regard the divine necessity of Jesus' death and third day resurrection as something totally devoid of meaning for their lives let alone for the world? Nevertheless, we in the World in Front of the Text are called and empowered to take our cues not from the negative, unbelieving reactions of others but from the positive response of these women to the truth of Jesus' *rhēma*. Indeed taken in conjunction with the ongoing responses to divine *rhēma* which have been traced from start to finish in the World of the Text, we in the World in front of the text have been equipped to understand how remembering divine *rhēma* involves:

- Remembering that with God not only is every utterance not impossible, but that which Jesus has uttered will be enacted;
- Remembering and sharing divine *rhēma* as did the women on the third day;
- Enacting Jesus *rhēma* as Simon Peter did one Galilean morning;
- Opening ourselves up to divine *rhēma* as the soon-to-be pregnant, teenage Mary did at Gabriel's annunciation.

Who knows where such remembering, believing, sharing, and enacting will lead the characters in the World of the Text and we characters who inhabit the World in Front of the Text? We may not always know where it will end, but whether in the World of the Text or the World in Front of the Text, we know where it begins: Every *rhēma* is not impossible for God!

Endnotes

1. For an excellent treatment of such reader and interpretive realities see the extended treatment given by Mark Allan Powell, *Chasing the Eastern Star: Adventures in Biblical Reader-Response Criticism* (Louisville: Westminster John Knox Press, 2001).

2. Details and treatments on various facets and dynamics of what is here being depicted as The World Behind the Text can be found in standard biblical introductions. Regarding New Testament introductions, for example, see the appropriate chapters in such works as Paul J. Achtemeier, Joel B. Green, Marianne Thompson, *Introducing the New Testament: Its Literature and Theology* (Grand Rapids, Michigan: Wm. B. Eedrmans Publishing Co., 2001); David A. deSilvan, *An Introduction to the New Testament: Context, Methods, and Ministry Formation* (Westmont, Illinois: IVP Academic, 2004); Bart D. Ehrman, *The New Testament: A Historical Introduction to the Early Christian Writings*, 4th ed. (New York: Oxford University Press, 2008); and Mark Allan Powell, *Introducing the New Testament: A Historical, Literary, and Theological Survey* (Grand Rapids: Baker Academic, 2009).

3. For examples of analyses in which the World of New Testament Texts is not just addressing but also seeking to subvert the standards of the World Behind the Text see Warren Carter, *John and Empire: Initial Explorations* (New York: T & T Clark International, 2008); idem, *Matthew and the Margins: A Sociopolitical and Religious Reading* (Maryknoll, New York: Orbis Books, 2000); Neil Elliott, *The Arrogance of Nations: Reading Romans in the Shadow of Empire, Paul in Critical Contexts* (Minneapolis: Fortress Press, 2008); Richard Horsley, *Hearing the Whole Story: The Politics of Plot in Mark's Gospel* (Louisville: Westminster John Knox, 2001); Richard Horsley, ed., *Paul and the Roman Imperial Order* (Harrisburg, Pennsylvania: Trinity Press, 2004); and Davina Lopez, *Apostle to the Conquered: Reimaging Paul's Mission, Paul in Critical Contexts* (Minneapolis: Fortress Press, 2008).

4   One example of such a confessional position regarding the ongoing interconnectivity between the Spirit, the World of the Text, and the World in Front of the Text may be found in the Confession of Faith of the Evangelical Lutheran Church in America which claims the following:

> The canonical Scriptures of the Old and New Testaments are the written Word of God. Inspired by God's Spirit speaking through their authors, they record and announce God's revelation centering in Jesus Christ. Through them God's Spirit speaks to us to create and sustain Christian faith and fellowship for service in the world.

Chapter 2: "Confession of Faith," in *Constitution, Bylaws, and Continuing Resolutions of the Evangelical Lutheran Church in America*, p. 19.

5   Of course the recognition of such an ongoing interconnectivity between the Spirit, the World of the Text, and the World in Front of the Text is not necessary in order to interpret the World of the Text itself. For example, one of the foremost New Testament scholars, Bart Ehrman, is a self-confessed agnostic who insightfully and regularly is able to investigate the World of the Text as an ancient writing without consideration of the Spirit's activity in speaking to the faith and life of the readers in the World in Front of the Text.

6   In the actual delivery of this Hein-Fry lecture, Luke 1:5-38 was introduced through a five-and-a-half minute PowerPoint presentation which integrated select music, artwork, and quotations from the biblical text in order to highlight some core components of these initial verses of Luke's theological narrative. In particular, the driving force in the World of the Text is the unleashing of God's plan which is now being fulfilled in the announcements of the births of John the Baptist and Jesus. Thus from the start of Luke's narrative, it is being established that God is going to accomplish what God plans to accomplish. Of related importance do this is the issue of where will humans stand in relationship to God's unfolding plan within the World of the Text. That is, because God will accomplish what God plans, will a person (or persons) reject that plan and so find themselves standing in opposition to God or will a person open themselves up to be a participant in and instruments for the accomplishment of God's plan. Subsequently in the World of the Text this issue is particularly highlighted in the speech of Gamaliel (Acts 5:33-39) and in the incredible turn of events involving Saul, Peter, and Cornelius as narrated in Acts 9–10.

7   See Joel B. Green, *The Gospel of Luke*, NICNT (Grand Rapids, Michigan: Wm. B. Eerdmans Publishing Co., 1997), 58-105.

8   All translations are those of the author.

9   Because contemporary English translations assume readers will not understand that the verb "to know" [γινωσκω/*ginōskō*] was an ancient euphemism for sexual intercourse, they erase this delicious linguistic and theological double entendre. Fortunately the four-century old King James Version retains the play on meanings of "know" which the World of the Text has intentionally constructed.

10 According to BDAG the two major possibilities of meaning for *rhēma* are "1 that which is said, word, saying, expression, or statement of any kind . . . 2 after

the Hebrew an event that can be spoken about, thing, object, matter, event..." BDAG, p. 905. Throughout this paper, *rhēma* will be regularly used to signal both its presence in the Greek text and its inherent polyvalent meaning.

[11] Luke's interactive focus between every *rhēma* not being impossible for God and characters opening themselves up to the divine *rhēma* is quickly reinforced in scenes related to Jesus' birth in Luke 2. Here the World of the Text uses *rhēma* in relationship to the responses of the shepherds and of Simeon to Jesus' birth:

- The shepherds were saying to each other, "Let us go to Bethlehem, and let us see this *rhēma* which has happened which the Lord made known to us."... When they saw, they made known the *rhēma* which was spoken to them about the child. (2:15,17)

- Simeon received the child into his arms and blessed God and said, "Now release your slave in peace, Lord, according to your *rhēma*" (2:28-29).

As was the case with Mary, both the shepherds and Simeon open themselves up to divine *rhēma* which has been disclosed to them and so join the celebration of salvation which is now dawning in the birth of Jesus in accord with God's plan.

[12] Green, *Gospel of Luke*, p. 232.

[13] The use of imperfect verb tenses (ηγνοουν/*ēgnooun* and εφοβουντο/*ephobounto*) in 9:45 intentionally stresses the ongoing nature of the disciples' inability to understand and their ongoing fear to ask Jesus about this *rhēma*. Likewise the use of a perfect, passive, periphrastic participle (ην παρακεκαλυμμενον/ *ēn parakekalummenon*) emphasizes that God has been the one continuously keeping this *rhēma* hidden from the disciples.

[14] 18:34 parallels 9:45 in using an imperfect verb tense (εγινωσκον/*eginōskon*) to stress the ongoing nature of the disciples not knowing the things which were being said and a perfect, passive, periphrastic participle (ην κεκρυμμενον/*ēn kekrummenon*) to emphasize that God was the one continuously keeping this *rhēma* concealed from the disciples.

[15] Also see related passion prophecies in 9:31,51; 13:31-35; 17:25; 21:9-19; 22:14-15,19-23.

[16] As Jesus had prophesied Judas hands him over to the religious leaders (22:47-53 fulfilling 22:21-22); the religious leaders reject Jesus and give him to Pilate who subsequently hands Jesus over to be crucified (22:66-23:1,24-25 fulfilling 9:22,44; 17:25; 18:32); and Jesus suffers crucifixion with two evil doers (23:32-46 fulfilling 9:22; 13:33;17:25; 18:32-33; 22:15,19-21,37-38,42).

[17] Note how the use of the verb δει/*dei* to depict the divine necessity of Jesus being handed over, crucified, and rising recalls its prior depictions of divine necessity in 2:49; 9:22; 13:33; 17:25; 22:37 and paves the way for such subsequent uses in 24:26,44.

[18] In 24:8,11 plural forms of *rhēma* are used to indicate that the women remembered the multiply times Jesus' had prophesied the divine necessity of his death and resurrection.

19 While the word *rhēma* appears only in 24:8,11 it is the implied antecedent of the pronoun ταυτα/*tauta* in 24:9,10. The translation has sought to show this by using "utterances" in the latter two verses.

20 Throughout Acts the importance of Jesus' resurrection and the resurrection of the dead will be stressed again and again (Acts 2:22-36; 3:12-22; 10:36-41; 13:26-39; 17:3,16-31; 23:6; 24:21; 26:6-8,19-23; 28:20).

21 The word rendered here as BS is the Greek word ληρος/*lēros* which is typically translated as "nonsense" (so NIV, NET, NJB) or "idle tale" (so RSV, KJB). This word, however, is much more charged than that. According to BDAG, ληρος/*lēros* refers to "that which is totally devoid of anything worthwhile" (p. 594). Here we have adopted David Lose's suggested translation to communicate the visceral, negative judgment which the apostles and other men render not just to the women's report but to the reality of Jesus' own *rhēma* regarding the divine necessity of his crucifixion and resurrection. David Lose, "Who's Afraid of an Empty Tomb," www.workingpreacher.org, posted 03.30.10.

22 BDAG, p. 594.

23 Note that as the women in this scene have been linked back to Mary via the uses of *rhēma* in 24:8-11; 1:38, the apostles and other men are linked back to Zechariah via their not believing in 24:11; 1:20.

Recovering the Bible as Oral Performances in Community

David Rhoads
Lutheran School of Theology at Chicago

Introduction

Near the close of his life, the noted Lutheran theologian, Joseph Sittler, shared with me his concern about the authority of the Bible. It was this: "People will not take the Bible seriously in our time just because someone says it is in the Bible. You will have to make it vital and alive." Those of us in biblical studies spend our careers trying to do just that, in a variety of ways. One way I have found to do this is to bring the biblical writings to life in oral presentations. I am convinced that incorporating such oral presentations into parish life will enliven the experience of the Bible in our time.

The writings in the New Testament were originally performed orally before communities of faith. What might we learn about these ancient performance experiences that can inform the way we experience the Bible in the parish today? The purpose of this lecture is to suggest that we can study the oral dynamics of the biblical writings in the early church as a way to invigorate the experience of the Bible in the twenty-first century.

This lecture is in three parts. First, I want to illustrate and explain the oral experience of New Testament compositions in the first century. Second, I will involve you in an experience of learning a biblical story by heart. Third, I want to explain some possibilities for oral storytelling in the context of the congregation. In the conclusion, I will reflect on the role that storytelling can take in dialogue with Scripture.

Part One: The New Testament as Oral Performances in the First Century.

How do we "recover" the oral dimensions of the New Testament compositions? We do not have video tapes or DVDs from the first century. We cannot get the sound back. We have no direct descriptions of performances of any of the New Testament writings. Nevertheless, we can get ideas from what we know of ancient storytelling and oratory. We can also get clues from the New Testament compositions themselves. After all, the writings we now have in the New Testament are transcripts of what were originally oral performances. Each was written to be performed. Letters were dictated orally for writing and then performed later for the communities to whom they were addressed. Gospels may have been composed and performed orally and then dictated and written down later.

Why do we say the compositions were originally performed orally? We think this is so because we know that the first century was a predominantly oral culture. Ninety-five percent or more of the people in the first century Mediterranean world were not able to read or write. The three to five percent who could read or write—mostly a small group of wealthy, powerful elites and their slaves—could do so with varying degrees of facility. All were steeped in a predominantly oral culture.

Before I say more about the orality of the first century and the New Testament writings, let me illustrate. I would like to perform the first seven or eight minutes of the Gospel of Mark (my translation). I use the term "perform" because we have every reason to think that the original New Testament compositions were most likely presented in lively and emotional ways by practiced storytellers and orators. Remember, first century followers of Jesus would have been eager to make the stories about Jesus vivid and meaningful. In this example, I am not trying to reproduce a performance of Mark in the first century. Rather, I am trying to make it meaningful and engaging in ways that might be familiar to us. [If you are reading this as an essay, please read the passage out loud and attempt to do so in a manner that is appropriate to the drama of the events being depicted]. Here it is:

> The beginning of the proclamation about Jesus the Messiah, the
> Son of God, just as it stands written in Isaiah the prophet:
> "Look, I am sending my ambassador ahead of you,
> who will pave the way for you,

> the voice of a herald in the desert,
>> "Prepare the way for the Lord,
>> Make his paths level."'"

It was John in the desert, baptizing people and calling for a repentance that leads to an amnesty for offenses. And the whole Judean countryside and all the Jerusalemites were going out to him and being baptized by him in the Jordan River, publicly acknowledging their offenses.

And John was wearing camel's hair with a leather belt around his waist, and he was eating grasshoppers and wild honey. And he was heralding, saying, "After me is coming one stronger than I am. I am not worthy to stoop down and untie the strap of his sandal. I baptized you in water, but he will baptize you in Holy Spirit."

And it happened—in those days Jesus came from Nazareth of Galilee and was baptized in the Jordan by John. And immediately coming up from the water, he saw the heavens being ripped open and the Spirit like a dove coming down onto him. And there was a voice from the heavens, "You are my only son. I delighted choosing you."

And immediately the Spirit drove him out into the desert, and he was in the desert forty days tested by Satan. And he was among the wild animals, and the angels were serving him.

Now after John was arrested and put in prison, Jesus came into Galilee with the proclamation about God, saying, "The opportune moment is upon us; the rulership of God has arrived. Turn around, and put faith in this gospel news."

And going along by the Sea of Galilee, he saw Simon and Andrew the brother of Simon casting nets in the sea, for they were fishermen. And Jesus said to them, "Come after me, and I'll make you become fishers of people." And immediately leaving the nets they followed him.

And going ahead a little further, he saw James the son of Zebedee and John his brother in the boat preparing the nets. And immediately he called them. And leaving their father Zebedee in the boat with the hired workers, they went off after him.

And they enter into Capernaum. And immediately on the Sabbath he entered into the synagogue and began teaching. And people were astounded by his teaching, for he was teaching them as one having authority and not like the legal experts.

And immediately there was in their synagogue a man with an unclean spirit. And it screamed out, saying, "What do you have against us, Jesus Nazarene? Did you come to destroy us? I know who you are—the holy one of God!"

And Jesus denounced it, saying, "Be quiet, and get out of him!" And the unclean spirit, convulsing the man and crying in a loud cry, came out of him.

And they were all so astonished that they were arguing with each other, saying, "What is this? A new teaching with authority? He commands even the unclean spirits and they obey him!" And the report about him immediately went out everywhere, into the whole surrounding countryside of Galilee.

And immediately coming out of the synagogue they went into the house of Simon and Andrew with James and John. Now Simon's mother-in-law was lying down with a fever, and immediately they tell him about her. And approaching her, he grasped her hand and raised her up. And the fever left her and she began serving them.

Now when it was evening, after the sun had set, people were bringing to him all the sick and the demon-possessed. And the whole city was gathered at the door. And he healed many who were sick with various illnesses and he drove out many demons. And he would not let the demons talk, because they knew him.

And early in the morning, while it was still quite dark, he arose, came out, and went off to a desert place and was there praying. And Simon and those with him tracked him down and found him, and they say to him, "Everyone's seeking you."

And he says to them, "Let's go elsewhere, to the next villages, so I might proclaim there too, for that's why I came out." And so he went proclaiming in their synagogues, in all Galilee, and driving out the demons.

I will stop here. Now I would like to invite you to speak in pairs about your experience of this oral presentation of the beginning of Mark and your reactions to it. If you are reading this as an essay, I invite you to reflect on the orality of your reading aloud. Please pose any questions you may have. They will help to prepare for the rest of the essay.

Now, having given you a performance experience of a portion of a New Testament composition, let me say more about what we think may have been the case with these oral performances in the first century.

First, we think that the New Testament compositions were originally experienced as oral letters and stories and not as Scripture. Hence, they came to people in a predominantly oral culture in the most familiar forms of speech: popular storytelling, oratorical speeches, and theater. As such, people probably did not think of a gospel or a letter as something written or as Scripture. Rather, they thought of them as a letter they heard performed by Timothy or Demos at a house meeting or as a gospel-telling event they witnessed in the market place in Thessalonica or Caesarea.

Second, the New Testament writings were not just "spoken" as though by a disembodied voice. They were "presented" as performances with vocal inflection, volume, facial expressions, gestures, and movement. This supposition is supported by first-century descriptions of orators and storytellers. It is also supported by clues in the texts themselves, because the stories themselves contain "stage directions" for the performer. Notice how often the story may say that someone "shouted" or "looked up" or "laid their hands" on someone. These are not only descriptions in the story; they are also directions to the performer to act the story out in a particular way.

Furthermore, there is good reason to think that even compositions as long as the gospels and letters were originally presented as a whole. People heard each of the gospels as a whole at one sitting, not broken up as we do by verses or lessons at worship. Mark takes a little more than two hours to perform, while the other gospels are somewhat longer, perhaps up to four hours. Apart from Romans, 1 and 2 Corinthians, and Hebrews, most letters in the New Testament take less than a half hour to perform. Revelation takes about an hour and forty-five minutes. Keeping these compositions in memory was not uncommon for a performer in an oral culture where memory was celebrated and nurtured. And experiencing a performance of such length was also not uncommon for an audience. It was the entertainment of the day. It was expected. Can you imagine someone today going to only the first half of a powerful film and then coming back later to see the rest? And can you imagine an ancient Christian community getting a letter from Paul and hearing only part of it?

Also, we think that when these compositions were written down, the purpose of the writing on the scroll was not to make multiple copies like a book for sale. Again, almost all the people did not read, and in any case the cost of a scroll was prohibitive. Rather, scribing a scroll was designed to assist a performer with memory work as they prepared for a performance or as they read it aloud. In ancient oral cultures, memory was more important than writing. As such, the manuscripts were simply repositories for the sounds, like musical scores. Besides, manuscripts had no features to aid in reading: no punctuation, no verse divisions, no paragraphs, no spaces between sentences, in fact no spaces between words, simply one letter after another for the whole scroll. You practically had to know the writing already by heart in order to read it with any facility! The main unit was the syllable, designed for vocal pronunciation. There was virtually no silent reading in the first century. You would read aloud to recover the sounds, just as you might hum aloud to a musical score as the means to "read" it. In an oral culture, sound was paramount, and the writing assisted performance.

Finally, there is every reason to think that the compositions were not read in private by individuals. Rather, they were performed for communities. They may have been performed in public spaces or community buildings or houses or synagogues that were open to the public or to a private group at a meal of celebration or in the context of a worshipping community. Communities experienced a New Testament composition collectively. And based on everything we know of audiences in this period, their responses were those of enthusiastic and lively audiences interacting with the performer.

What does all this mean? It means that the New Testament writings are examples of "performance literature." They are performance literature, like scripts for a drama or scores for a musical performance. They were intended to be performed. As such, the writings we have handed down to us are like fossil remains of what were once living performances. No, we cannot recover an original performance. Nevertheless, as I have suggested, we can learn about storytelling and speech making in the first century, and we can infer a lot from the compositions themselves. Mainly, however, we can reclaim the orality of the New Testament by telling these stories among ourselves as part of our Christian life together.

For two thousand years, we have lost the art and experience of the Bible as oral performance. We have read and studied the Bible as individuals in silence. Can you imagine a musicologist studying a musical composition silently and alone in a library without ever having heard a performance? Can you imagine a theater expert studying a script of a drama without ever having seen the play? Now, can you imagine that we Christians have been studying the Bible on the printed page and alone as individuals without ever having experienced a performance of even one of the biblical writings in its entirely at one time as a community? And when we do hear a small portion read in worship, the congregation is usually following along from a printed copy.

It is time to reclaim this oral experience of the performance of the Bible. To do this represents a major paradigm shift, because we will experience the Bible in a new medium of sound—as performers and as audiences. Several groups have already begun to spearhead this process. There is a movement among scholars called Biblical Performance Criticism that is helping scholars to interpret the biblical writings in fresh ways. Also, the Network of Biblical Storytellers holds storytelling festivals and fosters groups in local churches for learning and telling biblical stories. This paradigm shift to an oral medium has already begun to take hold in the academy, in classrooms, and in congregations.

This paradigm shift is timely in a culture that has for some time been moving beyond print—to television and the internet, to cell phones and email, to ipods and podcasts, and beyond. Performing the text is certainly one way, therefore, to bring the Bible into the twentieth-first century.

Part Two: Learn a Biblical Story

I am convinced that an experience of performance—both as performer and as audience—can offer new dimensions of engaging with the Bible. Now I would like to engage you in learning a story and telling it. With some guidance and direction, I invite you to learn a story from the Gospel of Mark, namely, a story about the encounter between Jesus and the Syrophoenician woman that results in the exorcism of her daughter.

Look below and you will see the story laid out in brief scenes showing the back and forth rhythm of the story. The back and forth scenario was originally composed this way to assist the performer in learning and remembering the story. I will speak each of the lines and ask you to repeat after me. Do not look at the text but simply listen and repeat as I lead you phrase by phrase. (If you are reading alone, read aloud with brief pauses between the parts.)

> *Jesus:* Now getting up from there, Jesus went off to the territory of Tyre, and he entered into a house because he did not want anyone to know he was there. But he could not escape notice.
>
>> *Woman:* Instead, a woman whose little daughter had an unclean spirit immediately heard about him, came, and threw herself at his feet. Now the woman was Greek, a Syrophoenician by birth! Yet she asked Jesus to drive the demon from her daughter.
>
> *Jesus:* But Jesus told her, "Let the children be satisfied first, for it isn't right to take the children's bread and toss it to the little dogs."
>
>> *Woman:* But she responded and said to him, "But, sir, even the puppies under the table get some of the little children's crumbs!"
>
> *Jesus:* And Jesus said to her, "Because of this word—go on off! The demon has gone from your daughter."
>
>> *Woman:* And when she went off to her house, she found the little girl resting on the bed—and the demon gone!

Now let me show you another step in learning and recalling a story. I want you to "imagine" the story as though it were happening before your eyes—by placing people and movements in a scenario. Again I will follow the back and forth movement that shifts the focus between Jesus and the woman.

> *Jesus:* Let's say this is Tyre over here off to the left side. Imagine that Jesus enters into a house to escape notice, but he cannot stay hidden.

Woman: Now see the woman come from her house from this direction to the right. She is not a Jew but a native Syrophoenician, a foreigner to Jesus. See her throw herself at Jesus' feet and beg for her daughter to be healed.

Jesus: Now imagine Jesus refusing her and calling her a dog for begging as she does. He refuses her with a saying that he will heal the Jews first before he heals non-Jews.

Woman: Now see how determined this woman is on behalf of her daughter. She cleverly turns Jesus' description of her as a dog by saying that even puppies get crumbs.

Jesus: Jesus is obviously surprised and moved by the woman's response. He changes his mind, and he tells her that the demon has gone from her daughter.

Woman: Finally, imagine the woman hurrying home back that way and finding her daughter freed from the demon and resting peacefully on the bed! What a wonderful outcome!

Now you have gone over the story. You have gotten oriented to it. You have even imagined it happening. You have "seen" it. The next step is to learn the story well enough to tell it. So I want you to take the next step and learn it by heart. I want you to do this in pairs. So turn and choose a partner and get ready to work together on this. (You can do this exercise also by yourself. Study it, tell it, then check, and repeat.) There are four steps to this process.

1. In pairs do the following exercise:

a. Read the passage silently and study it. Then have one person tell the story as closely as possible to the wording, while the other person listens without following along in the text. Then both of you look and see what was missed or added or changed. The purpose of this is to notice all the specific details of the text.

b. Repeat the above, but reverse roles.

c. When you have both finished, ask questions line by line without answering them. The purpose of this is to open up the story for exploration.

2. Now try another exercise that will help you get into this story and understand it.

Tell the story from the point of view of each character by changing the relevant pronouns. I recommend that you do this by reading it aloud to your partner (rather than trying to remember it) and let your partner simply listen without following along in the written text. To do this exercise, you do not need to write the story down with the changes. Just practice the story before you with the pronoun changes. Invest yourself in the feelings and tone of each character. When you have finished, talk together about the experience. Here is an example of how the story might be told by one of the characters.

> Now getting up from there, Jesus came to the territory of Tyre, and he entered into a house because he did not want anyone to know he was there. But he could not escape notice.
>
> Instead, I immediately heard about him. I have a daughter with an unclean spirit and so I came, and threw myself at his feet. Now I'm Greek, a Syrophoenician by birth. Yet I asked Jesus to drive the demon from my daughter.
>
> But Jesus told me, "Let the children be satisfied first, for it isn't right to take the children's bread and toss it to the little dogs."
>
> But I reacted and said to him, "But, sir, even the puppies under the table get some of the little children's crumbs!"
>
> And Jesus said to me, "Because of this word—go on off! The demon has gone from your daughter."
>
> And when I went off to my house, I found my little girl resting on the bed—and the demon gone!

You can see from this experience how the story is given new power and passion as you tell it from the first person point of view. This experience will help you get into the story and remember it better, because you have experienced the story from the point of view of the woman who so desperately wanted her daughter to be freed. Now change the pronouns again and let your partner tell the story from the point of view of Jesus. Perhaps you will also want to do it from the point of view of the daughter who was freed of the demon. Tell it as if this had happened for you! After each experience, reflect on what difference this makes to your understanding of the story and its impact on you.

3. The third part of this exercise will enable you to know and recall the story even more.

Follow the story, line by line, looking for the causation and connection between one line and the next. Ask how and why each line leads to the next line and follows the previous one. Put another way, ask why and how each thing said or done leads to the next thing said or done, and how it follows the previous thing said or done. This will help you trace the logic of the story from beginning to end. And it will assist memory, because each piece of dialogue or action will trigger your memory about what happens next.

4. By now you know the story quite well. Now is the time to nail it down in memory.

Learn each line in order. Learn each line one after the other by repeating it. Repeat the first line five or ten times without looking until you know it well. Then do the same with the next line. Then repeat both lines numerous times together without looking until you know them by heart. And so on, through the story. Then repeat the whole story until you know it by heart. To keep the story in memory, take opportunities to repeat it. To practice the memory work, repeat the words quickly. To practice *how* you will tell the story, slow down and concentrate on the meaning and power of the story. Then look for occasions to tell it to others.

Now you have learned a way to learn a story. Now we can talk about ways such stories that are in our hearts and minds can be shared in the context of congregational life.

Part Three: Bring Storytelling into the Life of the Congregation

There are many practical ways to incorporate oral presentation of the Bible into parish life. Note that we are not limiting the teaching and learning to a classroom. All aspects of parish life may be opportunities to teach and tell the biblical stories. I mention three examples here.

1. Bible class

Obviously a class could be taught in which teaching and conversation involve engagement with an oral performance of Scripture. The teacher can learn a story or text and perform it for the class. Or members of a class can take turns learning and presenting. Conversation and further teaching can follow. Because the group has had a common experience of the story, discussion follows more naturally. Note that the emotion of the telling and the identification with characters that happens will lead people to be personally involved in the story. A study of the lessons in the common lectionary each Sunday lends itself to this process. For longer pieces, you could view one of the performances of a biblical work on DVD.

2. Bible study/prayer group

Many congregations have storytelling prayer groups. Each time they meet, they learn a new story together. They might follow the group process described above or use other processes found in Tom Boomershine's book, *Story Journey*. Then during the time between meetings, they live with the story and are responsible for telling it to someone. On their return to the next meeting, they report how the story changed them or how it impacted others. There are many resources on the website of the Network of Biblical Storytellers (www.nbs.org) to establish such a group in your parish.

3. Scripture presentation at worship

Here is an opportunity for pastors and lay lectors to learn one or more of the lessons for each Sunday and to proclaim it. The preparation for this can be meaningful to the lector; and the telling of it makes the Scriptures a more powerful event in worship. Even if the lector reads the text, the preparation will assure that the reading is expressive and engaging. The website for the Go Tell organization (www.gotell.org) has guidelines and models for the readings for each week in the lectionary. In the Lenten season, some congregations assign brief passages of the passion narrative to many presenters for presentation as a whole.

Learning and telling Bible stories can also be meaningful in many other areas of parish life: pastoral counseling, hospital ministry, evangelism, social justice, youth ministries, vacation church school, among many others.

Conclusion: Transformation through Dialogue.

I would like to place this oral performance approach in the larger context of an understanding of teaching and learning. I like to think of the educational process as "transformation through dialogue." I believe the Spirit works as people engage in honest and meaningful dialogue with the Bible and with each other. It is even more transforming to engage the Bible with people of diverse perspectives from diverse social locations. One way to give the Bible a stronger voice in this dialogue is through learning it by heart, performing it for each other, and experiencing it orally as a community. In this way, the Bible now truly becomes one of the voices in the conversation, one of the dialogue partners. We experience a performance, and then we engage in dialogue. Then perhaps we hear the biblical "voice" again and talk further.

I have been performing biblical texts for my students, first in college and then in seminary, for over thirty years: the Gospel of Mark, the Sermon on the Mount, selections from Luke, scenes from John, Galatians, Philemon, James, I Peter, and the book of Revelation. It is a transforming experience for me to present and for my student to experience these compositions as performances. I have incorporated student memorization and performance in many classes. Students will learn a chapter of a Pauline letter or a story from one of the gospels to perform for their classmates. For many years, I have taught a course called "Scripture by Heart" in which students together present the birth stories of Luke or one of the passion narratives to the seminary community. In addition, each student learns a section of Scripture of their choosing to present to the community as a storytelling concert. This approach to teaching and learning has significantly changed my approach to education.

My experience has been that oral presentations of the text engender a more open interaction with the text. People experience it as if for the first time. They are led to notice things they have not previously noticed, to ask questions of all kinds, to express their feelings in relation to the characters and events, to identify diverse interpretations in response to the presentation, and to talk more readily about ways they personally connect with the story.

In this dialogue with the Bible and with each other, people may also be led to identify things in the stories that are problems for them. For example, in our story, we may ask: Why did Jesus call her a dog? How does it affect my understanding of Jesus that Jesus changed his mind? And that he did so in response to a gentle woman? What does it mean that Jesus healed someone who did not even believe in the God of Israel or that Jesus was the Messiah? What are demons, and how can we think about them today?

But also in this dialogue people may be open in new ways to be transformed: Does the story challenge us to repent of our exclusivism (as Jesus did!), and especially when there is cultural enmity as was the case here? Are we affected by the determination of this woman to get her child healed? Are we encouraged to be persistent in our requests for healing? Does the story lead us to listen to people on the margins (as Jesus did!)? Are we challenged to cross boundaries to bring the gospel to others? Are we empowered to embrace a healing ministry? Are we moved by the freeing of this little child from demonic powers.

Dialogue is an open conversation with the Bible and with each other. As such, people will agree and disagree about all these matters. In this dialogue, the role of a teacher is not to control the conversation or give answers or even to defend the Bible. Rather the role of the teacher is to be host and facilitator of the dialogue; to offer a safe, hospitable setting to perform and to listen; to have honest and open dialogue with the text and with each other; to avoid judgment and correction; to leave questions and consternations open so that the there is space for the Spirit to work; and to foster an openness to transformation.

In this context, the recovery of oral performances of the Bible places us in a whole new relationship with the Bible. Performing the text, experiencing the text in community, and engaging with it in dialogue may help us to invigorate teaching and learning the Bible in our time.

Selected Resources

Thomas Boomershine, *Story Journey* (Nashville: Abingdon, 1993). This is the key handbook for learning and telling biblical stories and for demonstrating their impact in congregational life.

www.gotell.org. This is a site that has oral presentations and performance commentary on each of the lessons in the church year.

www.nbs.org. This site has all the resources you will need to set up a storytelling group in your congregation as well as information about storytelling festivals throughout the country.

www.biblicalperformancecriticism.org. This site has many congregational and academic materials for understanding the Bible as oral performance in its own time and for furthering your commitment to experience the biblical writings as performer and audience today.

Learning the Bible in the Twenty-first Century
Lessons from Harry Potter and Vampires

Mary Hess
Luther Seminary

I am a Roman Catholic layperson, I teach at a Lutheran seminary in Minnesota, my research centers on digital media and faith, and at the moment my husband Eric and I are living and learning with our two sons—Nathaniel who is twelve and Alex who is seventeen.

All of these elements of my life contribute to how I see the world. I hope today to offer you some ideas that I have found helpful—but I offer them as moments that I hope invite you to your own analysis and provoke your own extended curiosity. I might sound like I am offering a specific prescription, but what I hope I am really offering is a way of seeing that will help you more adequately to construct a prescription for your own context.

Any of you who are yourselves young, or hang out with young people, will likely know that they are keen learners. Young people are amazingly good at ferreting out information that they are interested in. They are adept users of varieties of digital tools, and they are passionate about the people and ideas they care about.

On the other hand, precisely because of their abilities in these ways, when you present young people with the smorgasbord of options that is available in the twenty-first century U.S. context, it is very difficult to expand their interests beyond what they already enjoy.

Last spring the *Wall Street Journal* published a list of things workplace managers needed to understand if there were to manage successfully what the author called "the Facebook generation." The list had twelve elements on it:

1. All ideas compete on an equal footing.
2. Contribution counts for more than credentials.
3. Hierarchies are natural, not prescribed.
4. Leaders serve rather than preside.
5. Tasks are chosen, not assigned.
6. Groups are self-defining and self-organizing.
7. Resources get attracted, not allocated.
8. Power comes from sharing information, not hoarding it.
9. Opinions compound and decisions are peer-reviewed.
10. Users can veto most policy decisions.
11. Intrinsic rewards matter most.
12. Hackers are heroes.[1]

I have been involved in religious education for a long time, and in most of the places where I have worked, these characteristics are the opposite of how most churches organize learning.

So my first big idea for you today is that the question we need to engage in the church is *not* "how to" teach the Bible in the parish. Rather, the essential question is *why* to learn the Bible at all in the first place.

Why would a person want to learn the Bible?

There are certainly many rather negative answers offered up by churches: Things like: because it's the Word of God, and thus by implication, because I or we say so. Things like: because if you don't learn the Bible, you're going to hell. Things like: because every morally good person should know the Bible. Of course, these are not usually the explicit answers offered by churches, but rather more of the implicit curriculum that comes filtered through popular culture and other media.

I do not know about you, but I know that with my twelve year old these reasons do not work very well. In the first place, he is in a stage of his life where he is not convinced there even *is* a God. He is also clear that simply "because I say so" is not a valid reason. In part, I am to blame for that one, because I have worked hard to help him cultivate genuine skepticism in a world of competing beliefs.

As for the other reasons, while I believe Nathaniel truly desires to live a moral life, at this point I do not think it is because he is afraid of hell. In fact, given the extent to which he is attracted to TV shows like *Supernatural*, *Reaper*, and so on, I rather think his curiosity might lead him to inquire *more* about hell, rather than to avoid it.

We could draw a couple of conclusions from this that are sustained not simply by my anecdotal experiences with my children, but also from the scholarly research that is currently ongoing.

One of the key shifts that has taken place in the last couple of decades of research into teaching and learning is that scholars and educators have come to understand that we need to shift our attention from "teaching" to "learning." That is not to say that good teaching is no longer relevant or necessary—far from it! Rather, it is to note that we used to believe that there was something like "good teaching" that was universally applicable and consisted of a set of specific tools and practices.

Now we have grown to understand that good teachers design and sustain learning environments that are adaptive and geared to the specific learners found there. Good teachers are good improvisers, because at any given point in time the learners they are working with will come from very different contexts, very different backgrounds, with differing starting "databases" so to speak.

The title of one of my favorite books about adult learning makes this point directly. It is a book by Jane Vella entitled *Learning to Listen, Learning to Teach*.[2] Today in talking with you about teaching the Bible in the twenty-first century, I am going to focus on *learning* the Bible.

There are two main parts to this presentation, each of which is organized around a group of three words. In the first part I am going to explore the dynamics of "confirmation, contradiction, and continuity" as we think about learning the Bible amidst media culture. In the second part I am going to pick up the final piece of that first triad — continuity — and consider another triad within it, that of "authority, authenticity, and agency." By the time we are done, I hope to convince you that learning the Bible in the context we inhabit will require all of us to attend to these two triads, and will give us at least one powerful answer to "why" people might want to learn the Bible.

Confirmation, Contradiction, Continuity

Robert Kegan, a scholar whose work I respect enormously, believes transformative learning is a process of confirmation, contradiction, and continuity. Effective learning, he argues, begins with understanding where people are in their current frames of knowing.[3]

That is, in order to walk with someone on their learning journey, you must begin by understanding how they currently see the world. You must "confirm" the reality they are living. To return to the example of my twelve year old, the issue is not simply that he is uninterested in learning the Bible, it may also be that his current conceptions of the Bible are problematic. But before I can help him to understand something new, before I can help him to put together a more grounded and full notion of what it means to learn with and from and through the Bible, I need to start with where he currently is. I gain credibility and authority with him by being able to demonstrate that I know the world as he sees it.

This moment of seeking to discern the reality learners live in—what many educators would call a moment of assessment—is often the least engaged element of learning in the church.

Concretely speaking, if we want to help people *desire* to learn the Bible, it might help us to know something of what they currently think about the Bible. Given that my work centers on media culture, that is where I will take you.

There are biblical references—even actual engagements with the Bible—scattered all throughout popular culture. Here are a handful of video clips that may be familiar to you. Do this exercise with me. Find your handout, and the third page, where a linear spectrum is drawn. After each clip I show you, place the clip somewhere on that spectrum. Each clip is about three minutes long.

    a. "Fix the Bible" from Firefly, "Jaynestown," season 1, episode 7, 2002

    b. "The Bible is not a weapon" from Saved!, United Artists, directed by Brian Dannelly, 2004

    c. "Baracknophobia" from The Daily Show with Jon Stewart, 25 June 2008

    d. "Apt analogies" from The Simpsons, "She of little faith," season 13, episode 275, 2001[4]

So what did you discover? How did you decide what was real about a particular clip? What criteria did you use? Was it the genre? Was it the production values? Was it the message you felt the creator was conveying? Did it have anything to do with whether you felt manipulated or not?

Before we ever sit down with someone in a learning setting, or better yet, before we venture out to their contexts to learn with them, they already have an interpretive framework in their head with regard to media culture. That framework is deeply contextual, and what was most real for me, is likely *not* most real for you.

Each of these clips probably had something in them you could use to reinforce whatever you would like to teach about the Bible, but they probably also had things in them that you would like to contradict.

Perhaps our challenge with the Bible, and inviting people to learn with it, is not so much that they are not interested—perhaps it is that in fact people have already learned a lot about the Bible, and they are loathe to learn much more. It is not so much that the Bible does not matter to people or does not have an impact on them–it clearly does. Maybe part of the difficulty is that we, as educators in religious settings, want the Bible to matter to people *differently* from how it currently does, for different ends than it does, with different meaning than it does.

Confirmation is only the first step in learning. As Kegan notes, *contradiction* is a crucial element of learning. That is a moment when our meaning frames are cracked open in some way. Such contradiction, such cracking open, can happen simply through living. And it can happen when an educator enters the learning moment and poses some kind of specific problem, points out something previously unseen.

It is crucial for educators to understand where their learners are situated, the discursive terrain they inhabit; but it is perhaps even more important to think carefully about what kinds of contradictions live in that terrain, and what kind of contradictions need to be introduced.

One of the personal benefits for me of hanging around Lutherans as much as I do, is that I have been deeply steeped in a set of understandings about the Bible that open up possibilities beyond what we have just looked at in these pop culture clips.

Lutherans, for instance, frequently point out that Word of God has three very essential and intertwined meanings, only one of which is Scripture or the Bible. The first meaning of that phrase is Jesus Christ. That is, Jesus Christ is the Word of God incarnate. The second meaning of Word of God is what Lutheran Christians argue is the central proclamation of Christian faith: Law and Gospel. The third meaning is Holy Scripture, that is, the Bible.

Consider then, the implications that these three intertwined meanings have for understanding the Word of God in the Bible as represented in the video clips you just watched.

River's need to "fix" the Bible betrays her sense that it is a static, finished, somehow complete object—rather than a text of a community that is living, breathing, and still learning who God is, while the Shepherd Book can see how faith is a crucial element of engaging the Bible.

Word of God as Law and Gospel connects directly to our lived sense of sin and forgiveness. But that sense of what is sin and what is forgiveness can all too easily become a weapon in the hands of some, rather than an invitation. You can see this in the struggle both of the young people in the movie *Saved!* as well as in the late night satirical comedy show. What is God's promise? And how are we to understand what that promise calls us to?

Lisa Simpson's claim that the analogy is apt is a call from within the midst of "secular popdom" for a church that connects its Scripture with its living witness. Indeed, most of what is funny about that particular clip requires knowing the scriptural allusions; so simply "dressing up" the message is not deeply engaging it. Lisa uses the Bible itself to critique the situation.

How might we move towards creating learning environments that can help people live into these kinds of notions?

First, we have to foster a *desire* to learn more of the Bible; we have to find ways to be present where people live, to tap into their questions and yearning.

Second, we have to find ways to provide *compelling exploration* of the contradictions people inhabit, exploration that draws us into those contradictions, that does not seek to evade or avoid them.

Kegan notes, however, that there is a *final* piece to which we must attend—continuity. It is not enough to break open people's meaning frames through contradiction if we cannot at the same time offer them a new frame that still has continuity with the older one. Without that continuity, what often happens is what John Hull has called "premature ultimates"—bounded, stuck forms of knowing where people retreat into fortress mentalities or escape into relativistic disavowals.[5] How might we move from confirming our learners's reality to inviting them to see the contradictions present there? How do we do that while at the same time providing them enough continuity with their previous reality to walk forward faithfully in transformative ways?

Authority, Authenticity, Agency

There may be no more critical task in learning the Bible than this question of continuity, so I will focus on the challenge of providing continuity as people engage contradiction. To do this, I want to expand on continuity by bringing in the second triad I mentioned at the beginning of this essay, the elements of authority, authenticity, and agency. Let me give you two very brief illustrations of those elements.

For the first, go back to the list of Facebook culture attributes quoted at the start:

1. All ideas compete on an equal footing.
2. Contribution counts for more than credentials.
3. Hierarchies are natural, not prescribed.
4. Leaders serve rather than preside.
5. Tasks are chosen, not assigned.
6. Groups are self-defining and –organizing.
7. Resources get attracted, not allocated.
8. Power comes from sharing information, not hoarding it.
9. Opinions compound and decisions are peer-reviewed.
10. Users can veto most policy decisions.

11. Intrinsic rewards matter most.
12. Hackers are heroes.

Consider how each of these has to do with one or another of these dynamics. "All ideas compete on an equal footing" embodies shifting notions of authority. "Resources get attracted, not allocated" and "intrinsic rewards matter most" is about authenticity. "Tasks are chosen, not assigned" and "users can veto most policy decisions" are about agency. All three of these elements—authority, authenticity, agency—are shifting amidst media cultures.

Or another brief illustration would be the phenomenal success of the Harry Potter books. As various writers have pointed out, the books celebrate the critique of *authority*. They arrived during a cultural moment in which we are questioning received authority, questioning to some extent the world as we know it. So, too, does Harry, the chief character in the books, question the authority of the family he was fostered with, the teachers in his classrooms, even, eventually, Albus Dumbledore. In the process he has to come to grips with a world that has an entire dimension to it of which he was largely unaware. The books tap into our widespread sense of unease with what we can know; they give voice to our sense that there is more to this world than we have been able to identify.

We enter into this world of make-believe, and it comes alive in such a way as to show us something of ourselves in the process. The world J.K. Rowling describes *feels* real, it *feels authentic,* even though we know it is a fantasy, a story, make-believe. At the same time, kids being kids, there has been a tremendous amount of shared imagining with the world of the books taking place "off the page," if you will. Kids create websites. Kids dress up as Potter characters. Kids have *agency* in real time and real space—not to mention that the characters of the books themselves demonstrate a kind of agency in the story that is more powerful than that of mere muggles.

Three elements: Authority, authenticity, agency. The shifts these elements of authority, authenticity, and agency are undergoing hold both promise and challenge to those of us in religious community. They also are a particular key to the puzzle of what it means to provide continuity.

Let me take the first one, authority, and give you an extended example of what I mean when I suggest that engaging shifts in authority is necessary to supporting learning the Bible. Engaging shifts in authority directly can help to provide the kind of continuity that can draw learners beyond contradiction. Let's talk, for instance, about an assertion we could make, that the Bible creates community and therefore is best understood in community. This is not how our wider culture represents the Bible. Many people believe the opposite: that the Bible is something best understood personally, in individual devotion. Or, alternatively, rather than the Bible *creating* community, many people believe that the Bible provokes divisiveness, that the Bible foments conflict, it *divides* community.

To argue that the Bible creates community is to make a claim which sharply contradicts some learners' reality. There is a natural tendency for learners to want to draw back in one of two ways in engaging such contradiction. One tendency is to accept that the Bible creates community, and then to assume that that community is narrowly construed and strictly defined. This is the path that leads towards fundamentalism. It offers a "premature ultimate" that creates rigidly defined identity boundaries. A second tendency, which might at first seem to be the opposite, is to reject the claim that the Bible creates community all together and hold onto individualized, privatized forms of religious knowing. In this case, everything becomes relative. The Bible's meanings are understood individually and privately. What I take from the Bible is what I take from it, and what you take from it is equally true — for you — even if the meanings contradict each other. This is the path that leads toward relativism.

To get beyond either of these responses to the contradiction, however, we need to find, to provide, to offer, to glean *continuity* in the face of the contradiction. Something from our previous form of understanding needs to be connected to a new frame that resolves the contradiction. In this example, I think we can offer continuity by drawing deeply from the wells of personal experience that emerge from shared learning. Communal forms of knowing, even the most basic participatory forms, have both resonance and dissonance with shifting notions of authority. They have resonance if authority is understood as *emerging from* but not wholly *constrained by* that community. They have dissonance, however, if the flattening of authority is understood primarily as heightening individual authority, heightening individualist forms of knowing.

One of the stronger claims that Christians make is that the Bible is best understood in community. It is not simply a book for individuals. The

Word of God is for all. From the earliest texts of God's promises to the descendants of Abraham and Sarah, to letters that Paul and other early Christians shared in the context of spreading the news of Jesus, these are texts that are *of and for community*. They are God's story, God's story of relationship with human beings.

When we share ideas about the Bible, when we try to teach—and thus support learning—we need to be aware, consciously and consistently, of understanding *authority* in community-oriented ways, but community-oriented ways that draw out new meaning, rather than closing it down.

One of the real challenges we face in teaching the Bible is that in the church we have not consciously designed learning in that way.

Consider this set of diagrams.[6]

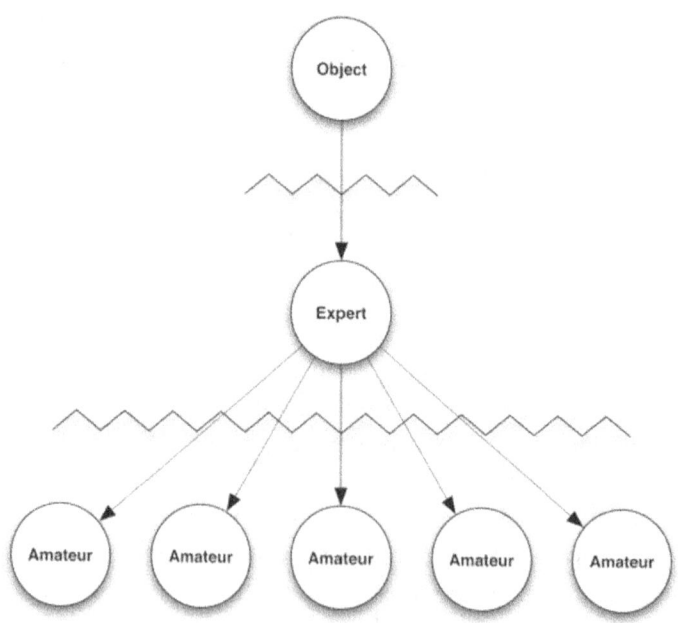

In this one, taken from Parker Palmer's book *The Courage to Teach*, knowing is depicted as information that is transferred from an object by an expert to a group of amateurs.

The movement of information is unilinear, that is, it goes in only one direction. It may seem more efficient—certainly, if the information does not get to the amateurs there is clearly someone to hold accountable—but is efficiency what we are aiming for?

On the other hand, here is a different way of thinking about it.

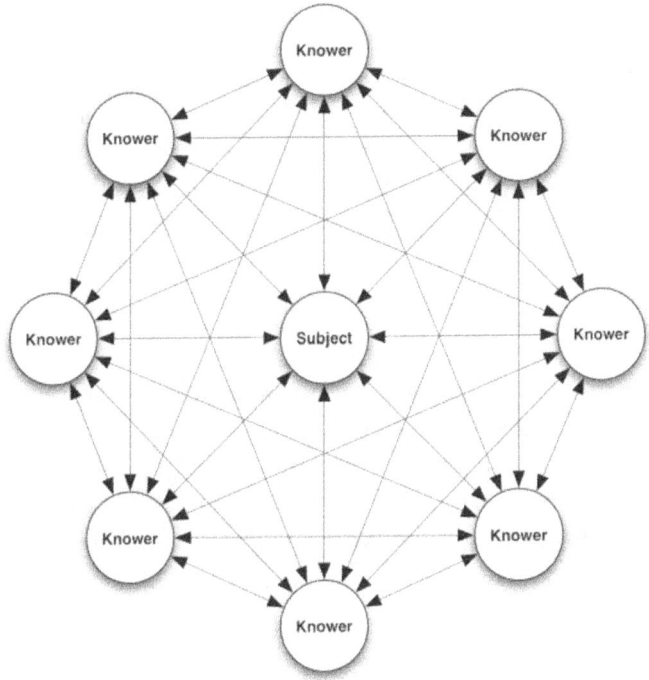

In this diagram Palmer shows the learners gathered around the subject to be known. Each learner has a direct connection with that subject—and indeed, "subject" is a much more descriptive term for active engagement—and each learner has a relationship with each other. So the knowing builds from the community. Indeed, the more knowers are involved, the more robust the knowing.

Now, if you are like many of the other groups with whom I have spoken, you are probably asking yourself: Where is the teacher in this diagram? Is the teacher simply one of the many knowers? Certainly every teacher must be also a learner, but I would argue that the teacher in this diagram is invisible. The teacher is the person or persons who are designing the environment so as to allow each learner to stay in direct contact with the subject, as well as in shared relationship with each other. The teacher is the person who makes sure that the ignorance of one person does not become shared ignorance or that the assertions of one person do not silence the knowing of others. The teacher ensures that learners stay in direct relationship with the subject at the heart of it all. Palmer notes that "to teach is to create a space in which obedience to the truth is practiced."[7]

When we teach in this way, when our patterns better match the second diagram, learners come to understand that authority and credibility are built up, are created and shared, not simply presumed, assumed, or imposed. As the Wall Street Journal piece I quoted earlier noted, "ideas compete on an equal footing" and "hierarchies are natural not prescribed." What does that mean here? It means that if we start from where people are in relation to the Bible and we work from there, we do our best work by inviting the most robust and diverse group of conversants into the conversation that we can.

We practice Bible study, for instance, as a means of listening and hospitality. As my colleague Rolf Jacobson noted last summer at the Book of Faith jubilee event held prior to the churchwide assembly, when we look for leaders/teachers of Bible study, we ought to be looking for leaders whose gift is that of hospitality. We create shared authority by supporting *relationality*. In doing so we are also creating *continuity* for learners. We are inviting them to understand experientially that there is deep *personal* connection to their knowing of the Bible *and* there is deep *communal* knowing. They have an experience in which they can be drawn beyond the dichotomies of either fundamentalism or relativism. This is an example of creating continuity by addressing the realm of *authority*.

What about authenticity? How might we provide continuity through engaging with dynamics of authenticity? In media culture, as Thomas Boomershine once noted, we tend to reason by means of sympathetic identification rather than philosophical argument.[8] We *feel* our way through a story, we find a particular movie compelling because it *feels* authentic. But what constitutes "authenticity"? One component has to do with congruence between our feelings and our expectations and experiences. In feeling our way through situations, do our feelings resonate, do they match our previous experiences and our expectations?

This is an element of media cultures which can be very perplexing, because on the one hand our media provide a seemingly endless variety of stories into which to be drawn, into which our experiences can be tuned.

Yet on the other hand that endless variety is actually fairly narrowly circumscribed. We find ourselves flooded by media in which stories are told and we are invited to "feel with" various characters, but the key question might well be whether this "feeling with" enlarges us or narrows us.

Which brings me to the world of vampires. Unless you have been completely isolated from popular culture, you know that vampires, zombies, and other denizens of the undead imagination are particularly prevalent in pop culture right now. Guillermo del Toro and Chuck Hogan had a beautifully argued piece in *The New York Times* reflecting on this phenomenon. They write that:

> In other words, whereas other monsters emphasize what is mortal in us, the vampire emphasizes the eternal in us. Through the panacea of its blood it turns the lead of our toxic flesh into golden matter.
>
> In a society that moves as fast as ours, where every week a new "blockbuster" must be enthroned at the box office, or where idols are fabricated by consensus every new television season, the promise of something everlasting, something truly eternal, holds a special allure. [9]

This is an argument that I find deeply intriguing. Those of us who confess a God who grants us eternity on the basis of faith ought to be paying attention to elements of this argument. What is the *feeling* we might confirm here? Surely we do not wish to confirm the reality of vampires and zombies—whose very fantasmic nonreality is probably also part of their attraction—but what about the underlying emotion, the desire for something that lasts, for eternity, that might be expressed in our fascination with vampire stories?

Del Toro and Hogan go on:

> Part of the reason for the great success of "Dracula" is generally acknowledged to be its appearance at a time of great technological revolution. . . . Today as well, we stand at the rich uncertain dawn of a new level of scientific innovation. . . . Our technological arrogance mirrors more and more the Wellsian dystopia of dissatisfaction, while allowing us to feel safe and connected at all times. We can call, see, or hear al-

most anything and anyone no matter where we are. For most people then, the only remote place remains within. "Know thyself" we do not.[10]

Yet "know thyself" is a fundamental element of Christian faith. "Love thy neighbor as thyself" suggests a demand to know something of who one is. I believe that our embodiment teaches us something about an incarnational God, and our ability to attend to that embodiment, in all of its rich, confusing, and complex diversity, is a key to thoughtful theology. More and more of popular culture is infused with searching and wandering and *feeling* on themes that are at the heart of Christian faith.

Before you begin to think, however, that I am simply an apologist for popular culture, someone who accepts any and all things that flourish there, remember that I am exploring contradictions so as to also ponder what kinds of continuity learning the Bible might offer us.

Sympathetic identification is a process of "feeling with." There is much in religious community which invites "feeling with," but I would argue that what we are actually seeking in faith, in Christian community, and thus in learning the Bible is not so much "sympathetic identification" as it is "empathetic identification." The continuity we have to offer when we engage authenticity comes from stretching beyond sympathy to empathy. When we claim deeply embodied knowing, deeply embodied "feeling with," we need to always link that knowing within community. Sympathy involves using your own experiences to "feel with" someone else. Although it involves an "other," sympathy does not stretch beyond oneself; it is still profoundly self-centered. Empathy, on the other hand, involves being able to feel with another even if one has *never* had the same experience, and even if the experience places one's own experiences in a different light. Empathy invites and involves self-differentiation and compassion that is other-oriented.

You can see the distinction between sympathy and empathy at work in many Bible stories. Jesus is asked, "Who is my neighbor?" and his reply is that we are called to love our enemies (Luke 10:29). The "trick" or "turn" of many of the parables is that a listener often identifies with a particular character, only to discover that the story rewards a different one. In the parable of the workers in the vineyard (Matthew 20) *every* worker is paid the same, even the ones who only worked towards the end of the day. Hearing that story we wonder, along with the characters who worked all day, "Shouldn't we be paid more because we worked longer?" That's a question arising from *sympathetic identification*. Feeling, on the other hand, that everyone should be paid the same regardless of how many hours worked—that is a feeling that might grow out of an empathic sense that a worker who spent most of the day waiting to work *without* hope, *suffered* in doing so. Or, perhaps, that all are entitled to share in common the abundance being offered.

Parables are a specific form of narrative in the Christian tradition, and as Anderson/Foley note:

> Parabolic narratives show the seams and edges of the myths we fashion. Parables show the fault lines beneath the comfortable surfaces of the worlds we build for ourselves. Myth may give stability to our story, but parables are agents of change and sometimes disruption.[11]

Anderson and Foley are giving different language to the same dynamic I have been tracing. You might say that the "mythic provides continuity" while the "parabolic creates contradictions."

The reality that much of media culture invites sympathetic identification, then, is not so much an impossible obstacle to Christian storying, as it is a first step and an invitation. The Bible demands *empathy*, but our wider contexts teach us *sympathy*. This contradiction is particularly evident within the narrative forms most prevalent in mediated spaces. Unfortunately, certain constrained versions of Christian identity actually limit the development of empathy by closing down invitations to experience "otherness" as a means towards transformation. Perhaps the most obvious example of this constriction might be the response of several Christian communities to *Harry Potter*. In part because the novels have central characters who are witches and wizards, these Christian communities argue that their children should not be allowed to read the books, for fear of contamination. One element of that fear is risking identification with an "other" who is far outside the bounds of one's own community.

Yet empathy is a form of identification that does not merge. In other words, one can empathize with someone else *without becoming* that other. Sympathy, on the other hand, invites identification through a kind of self-centeredness.

So, too, the challenge of representing homosexuality in positive ways in mass media. Many progressive Christians champion such portrayals, believing that in inviting sympathetic identification, such media representations hasten change. But sympathetic identification is not what the gospel commands. *Empathy* is what is demanded. So while progressive Christians might celebrate these portrayals for confirming their own beliefs, the deeper call to such Christians really ought to be one of being drawn into relationship with those who *condemn* homosexuality, precisely because the gospel calls us to love those from whom we are estranged, those who are strangers to us, even enemies.

Similarly, many conservative Christians fear positive portrayals of gays and lesbians in part because they fear people might identify with them, and perhaps even "become" them. Such a fear ignores the scientific research that being gay is not a choice, but rather a given. But it also ignores the possibility of being able to empathize with someone who is very different from you, without in some way *becoming* that person. Even the most conservative of Christian communities ought to be able to find ways into *empathy* with those who are different.

There is another lesson in the stories of vampires. Many of them — I like Octavia Butler's book *Fledgling*, for instance — explore what it feels like to be drawn into relationship with someone of whom you are deeply frightened, only to discover a relationship that arises even while the differences do not go away. To provide continuity past the contradictions of "feeling with," to provide continuity that allows an authenticity bigger than similarity, we have to stretch into empathy — an invitation the Bible makes over and over again.

So what does this mean for religious educators? For local churches? For learning the Bible? We need to think about all the learning we are engaged in, in terms of stretching sympathetic identification into empathetic identification. We need to help people draw on their own experiences as a way into community, but not into sameness. Learning with the Bible can do this.

I have spoken now about *providing continuity through engaging experiences of shared authority*, or participatory knowing. And I have spoken about *providing continuity through deepening authenticity from sympathy into empathy*. Let me continue to the third element, that of agency.

Agency has to do with whether persons feel like they are able to "make a difference," are able to "have an impact." In the United States it is common to see action on pressing issues represented in fairly individualistic ways. Indeed, careful examination of the ways in which newscasts represent action leads to the conclusion that agency is overwhelmingly represented as a function of consumption, or at least of individual action through circulation of funds. A powerful example would be responses to the earthquake in Haiti. People view the earthquake damage on television, and they are invited to send money to relief organizations.

The systemic underlying poverty that exists in Haiti, the lack of infrastructure and a functioning government, makes the challenge of recovery far greater than anything funding alone can accomplish. Of course for Haiti to recover, more funds *will* be necessary. But where are the calls for Americans to change the structural financial relationship between Haiti and the world? Where are the calls to cancel all debt? To let any Haitian who can reach us, come into the U.S. as a refugee? Only very slowly, if at all, are people raising these issues. We are *not accustomed* to thinking in communal, structural, systemic terms when we think of agency. Instead, we have been socialized into thinking in terms of spending funds, accumulating funds, and other primarily individual responses.

It is not surprising that many people understand *consumption* as their primary means of agency when that is what the media show us. I am not seeking to condemn consumption (or limiting one's consumption) as a form of action, rather I am seeking to call attention to the dilemma that *only* representing agency in that way is highly problematic for religious communities.

For millennia religious communities have conceived of *agency* as an attribute of humanity which is granted by, empowered through, God. Differing theologies will describe such agency in different ways, but one example would be a belief that God is at work in the world and human beings share in that action as elements of God's ongoing creative activity. The Bible begins and ends with the agency of God. While individual human beings do indeed make individual human choices and take individual human action in Bible stories, much of the time the action that is individually oriented—or even more so, only about consumption—has devastating consequences.

Given such an understanding, it is highly problematic for communities of faith to reinforce notions of agency through consumption, yet that is precisely what many of us are doing. In the U.S. we have a huge industry devoted to producing Christian "stuff"–everything from books and movies, to music, clothing, household goods, and so on. While it is also true that some Christian communities have begun to focus on lowering consumption—particularly as a means of easing global climate change—far too many of us continue to perceive agency in this individualized way.

Weaving Our Story with God's Story

What are our alternatives?

Traditionally we have posed alternatives through practices of communal worship—corporate prayer and communal discernment, for instance. Recently there has been a movement growing in the U.S. around notions of "practices of faith" that has highlighted a number of other such forms of action: testimony, discernment, healing, singing, and so on. In these practices it is God's agency that is clearly highlighted, while human agency is intimately connected to God *through community*.[12] The reality is that many of these practices are increasingly unfamiliar to people, even those who do have a vibrant faith community accessible to them.

One of the gifts, for me, of the media literacy movement has been learning that the best way to help people become literate—really what we mean is "fluent"— in media, is not by teaching them how to critically interpret various media, but rather by helping them to create in various media. That is, kids learn far more about media framing by attempting to create their own videos, then by being told how to "view" specific media. They become critics in the process of learning how to create in a specific medium.

Thus if we are going to "contradict" the notion that individual agency is tied to practices of consumption, and offer a larger view of God's agency creating in our midst, of God's mission in the world through our hands, our hearts, our eyes, then we have to find ways for people to tell their stories as bound up with God's story. We cannot simply pound into them that this is God's story, we have to invite them to discover in their own stories, and in the stories of the communities of which they are a part, and the communities which empathy invites them to engage, *God's story*.

We need to be creating learning environments in which we ask learners to ponder questions like:
- What do you/we think God is doing here?
- What do you/we hear God saying personally, to you?
- What do you/we hear God saying to us?

We need to ask those questions not simply or only of biblical texts, but also and perhaps even more often, of the media culture stories all around us. And we need to engage each other's responses *in community* not in isolation. As we are learning with the Bible, we should be able to help each other live in a God-saturated world. And if we are doing THAT well, than the empathy that grows will be fundamentally transformative of the world we live in; and the authority we create will be more sustaining and generative.

I started by telling you stories of my twelve year old, Nathaniel. Let me begin to close by noting that to date he has been most fascinated—when it comes to learning the Bible—by the sections of the *Lutheran Handbook* that talk about the seven funniest Bible stories, the five grossest Bible stories, and so on.[13] I am working to find ways to meet him where he lives, where his primary reality is defined, and to draw him both more deeply into that and beyond it. Rather than avoiding popular culture because we fear diluting or contaminating biblical learning, we need to figure out where people's desires and curiosities are residing, and find ways to connect them with the deep stories and vivid poetry of the Bible.

But as we do so, we need to be continually alert—as educational leaders, as pastoral leaders—to the mythic/parabolic dialectic, to the contradiction/continuity dynamic. We need to focus on developing empathy, not simply sympathy. And we need to do so in ways that help people weave their own stories with God's story.

If we really take seriously the Bible as the Word of God, if we really believe that God is continuing to act in our midst, then we need to be alert and listening all around us, not only to those voices who claim–often on their own authority and their own behalf–that they are authoritative voices for God, but also to all those other voices, particularly, perhaps, those voices who seem most distant. We need to meet our learners where they live. We need to draw them more deeply into the contradictions they are experiencing. And we need to move together, into our shared story.

Confirm. Contradict. Continue.

Authorize. Authenticate. Take action.

Why learn the Bible? Because it tells us who we are, and who we can become.

Endnotes

1. Gary Hamel, Wall Street Journal blog Management 2.0 (retrieved from http://blogs.wsj.com/management/2009/03/24/the-facebook-generation-vs-the-fortune-500/ on 3 September 2010).

2. Jane Vella, *Learning to Listen, Learning to Teach* (San Franciso: JosseyBass, 2002).

3. See both Robert Kegan, *The Evolving Self* (Cambridge, Massachusetts: Harvard University Press, 1982), and Robert Kegan, *In Over Our Heads* (Cambridge, Massachusetts: Harvard University Press, 1998).

4. Video excerpts from the following: Firefly (Season 1, Episode 7, "Jaynestown," first aired on Fox, October 2002). Saved! (United Artists, 2004). The Daily Show (Episode 13085, "Baracknophobia," first aired on the Comedy Channel, June 25, 2008). The Simpsons (Season 13, Episode 275, "She of little faith," first aired December 16, 2001.

5. John Hull, *What Prevents Christian Adults from Learning?* (Philadelphia: Trinity Press International, 1991).

6. Epistemological diagrams from Parker Palmer, *The Courage to Teach* (San Francisco: JosseyBass, 1998), figures 4.1 "the objectivist myth of truth," and 4.2 "the community of truth."

7. Parker Palmer, *To Know As We Are Known* (San Francisco: HarperOne, 1993), 88.

8. Thomas Boomershine, "How to be a faith witness in the communications media? Conditions requisite for the public communications value of faith witnesses," paper presented at the Witnessing to the Faith, An Activity of the Media conference, St. Paul University, Ottawa, Ontario, May 30, 1999.

9. Guillermo del Toro and Chuck Hogan, "Why Vampires Never Die," Op-Ed, *The New York Times* (July 30, 2009) (retrieved from http://www.nytimes.com/2009/07/31/opinion/31deltoro.html on 3 September 2010).

10. *Ibid.*

11. Herbert Anderson and Edward Foley, *Mighty Stories, Dangerous Rituals* (San Francisco: Jossey-Bass, 2001), 14.

12. See, in particular, Dorothy Bass, ed., *Practicing Our Faith* (San Francisco: Jossey-

Bass, 1997) and Bass and Dykstra, eds., *For Life Abundant* (Grand Rapids, Michigan: Wm. B. Eerdmans Publishing Co., 2008); as well as the website www.practicingourfaith.org.

[13] Skrade and Satter, eds., *The Lutheran Handbook* (Minneapolis: Augsburg Fortress Publishers, 2005).

The Lecturers

Richard Carlson

Richard Carlson serves as the Philip H. and Amanda E. Glatfelter Professor of New Testament Language, Literature, and Theology at the Lutheran Theological Seminary, Gettysburg, Pennsylvania. His primary area of teaching is New Testament studies as well as Greek. He is also serving as the seminary's acting director of internship. A native of Minnesota, Dr. Carlson holds degrees from Concordia College in Moorhead, Minnesota; Wartburg Theological Seminary in Dubuque, Iowa; and Union Theological Seminary in Virginia. Prior to joining the faculty at Gettysburg in 1990, he served pastorates in northern Minnesota. Dr. Carlson has published material on the New Testament and its relationship to such areas as New Testament exegesis, preaching, Jewish-Christian relationships, diaconal ministry, evangelism and ministry in the twenty-first century, and baptism. His books are *Preaching 1 Corinthians 13* (co-authored and edited with Dr. Susan Hedahl) and *New Proclamation, Year C, 2004, Easter through Pentecost*. Dr. Carlson has three children, who lead their own very active lives. He is married to the Rev. Dr. Michelle Holley Carlson.

Susan Briehl

Susan Briehl, a Lutheran pastor, has served as director of Holden Village, a Lutheran center for renewal in the North Cascade Mountains, campus pastor at Pacific Lutheran University, and pastor of Our Saviour's Lutheran Church in Bellingham, Washington. Currently, she is a member of the Indiana-Kentucky Synod (ELCA), called to her work with the Valparaiso Project on the Education and Formation of People in Faith (www.practicingourfaith.org). Susan's work includes "Food" and "Study," co-authored with her daughters Mary Emily and Magdalena, in *Way to Live: Christian Practices for Teens* (Upper Room, 2002); "Living in the Presence of God" in *On Our Way: Christian Practices for Living a Whole Life* (Upper Room, 2010), co-edited with Dorothy C. Bass; *Holden Prayer Around the Cross* (Augsburg, 2010), written with Tom Witt; and *Turn My Heart: A Sacred Journey from Brokenness to Healing* (GIA, 2003) and *Unfailing Light: An Evening Setting of Holy Communion* (GIA, 2004), both written with Marty Haugen. She has authored several hymn texts, including "Holy God, Holy and Glorious." Susan lives in Spokane with her husband, Martin Wells.

Mary Hess

Mary Hess joined the Luther Seminary faculty in July of 2000. Hess received her B.A. in American Studies in 1985 from Yale University in New Haven, Connecticut. She received her M.T.S. degree in 1992 from Harvard University in Cambridge, Mass. In 1998 she received her Ph.D. in religion and education from Boston College in Chestnut Hill, Massachusetts. Hess' most recent professional experience includes serving on the editorial board of the premier journal in her field, *Religious Education* (1999-present), working with the Lexington Seminar and the Wabash Center, and serving as a core member of the International Study Commission on Media, Religion and Culture. She is a member of the Religious Education Association, the American Academy of Religion, and the Catholic Theological Society of America. Her most recent publications include the books: *Teaching Reflectively in Theological Contexts: Promises and Contradictions* (Melbourne, Florida: Krieger, 2008), and *Engaging Technology in Theological Education: All That We Can't Leave Behind* (New York: Rowman Littlefield, 2005). She maintains her own website and has written her weblog, Tensegrities, since 2003.

David Rhoads

David M. Rhoads is emeritus professor of New Testament at the Lutheran School of Theology at Chicago. Ordained in 1968, Rhoads was pastor of St. John Lutheran Church, Asheboro, North Carolina (1968-1970), and professor of religion at Carthage College, Kenosha, Wisconsin (1963-1968), before joining the seminary faculty in 1988. He is married to the Rev. Sandra Roberts. He has two children and five grandchildren, two of whom he and Sandra raise, and one great-grandchild. They live in Racine, Wisconsin. Widely published, Rhoads is an accomplished oral interpreter of biblical writings that include the Gospel of Mark, the Sermon on the Mount, Galatians, James, 1 Peter, and the book of Revelation. He is the author of several books including *Mark as Story: An Introduction to the Narrative of a Gospel* (Fortress Press, 1999) and *The Challenge of Diversity: The Witness of Paul and the Gospels* (Fortress, 1996). In 2004, he published a collection of his essays, *Reading Mark, Engaging the Gospel.* In addition, he has taught in the Select program of video courses for continuing theological education. An enthusiastic environmentalist, Rhoads was advisor to the seminary's Green Zone Committee and has planned eco-conferences, edited guidebooks for parishes, and helped initiate "The Web of Creation," an online environmental service for congregations (www.webofcreation.org). Rhoads also recently wrote *The Green Congregation Training Manual*, and with David Glover, *An Environmental Guide for Churches, Their Buildings and Grounds.* Both are available online at www.webofcreation.org. He now also directs the Green Congregation Program, which works primarily with clusters of congregations in some Midwest synods of the ELCA. In 2007 he edited a collection of sermons by thirty-six different theologians and preachers, *Earth and Word: Classic Sermons on Saving the Planet* (Continuum, 2007).

Margaret A. Krych

Margaret A. Krych is the Charles F. Norton Professor Emerita of Christian Education and Theology at the Lutheran Theological Seminary at Philadelphia. She retired in 2008 after thirty-one years at the seminary where she was associate dean of graduate education (directing the master of sacred theology, doctor of ministry, and doctor of philosophy degree programs), and where she taught courses at professional and graduate level in Christian education and theology. Her many publications include *Teaching the Gospel Today* (Augsburg, 1987), *Teaching About Lutheranism* (Augsburg Fortress, 1993), *The Ministry of Children's Education: Foundations, Contexts, and Practices* (Fortress Press, 2004), and "The Bible and Those Difficult Topics," *Parish Teacher*, Vol. 19:4, December 1995, pages 2-3. She is an ordained minister of the Evangelical Lutheran Church in America and has served on several boards and churchwide committees of the ELCA. She is married to a retired, ordained Lutheran minister and lives in a suburb of Philadelphia. They have two adult children.

Laurie Jungling

Laurie Jungling is assistant professor in the religion department at Augustana College, Sioux Falls, South Dakota. She teaches courses in Christian ethics, Christian theology, and introductory religion. She is interested in the Lutheran concept of vocation as a positive framework for engaging difficult moral issues, particularly issues surrounding sexuality. Dr. Jungling received her Ph.D. from the Graduate Theological Union and is an ordained pastor in the Evangelical Lutheran Church in America.